HACKING YOUR DESTINY

Karl Lillrud

ISBN: 978-1-951503-19-2 (Ebook)
ISBN: 978-1-951503-18-5 (Paperback)

\\\ AUTHORSUNITE

Published by Authorsunite.com

Introduction

Why you should read this book and what it is about:

This book is about an entrepreneur's quest for answers; answers that when being asked and thought about, could be found within one's self. I believe you will enjoy it no matter who you are, and at what place you are in your life.

It's written in a way to inspire and educate you, the reader, to be supportive, competitive, challenging, and fun. It will give you a new perspective on life and I assure you that you will learn how to improve and get more out of your life.

Why I wrote this book:

It all started with a closed community talk for entrepreneurs called 'Zynergy talks'. In my quest to write a speech on 'outside-the-box' thinking, I found myself wildly riddled with deep feelings and questions; constantly arguing with myself as I was searching for answers. Instead of just accepting things as they were and moving on as most people I know would, I started to think back on my life to find out why I was operating the way I did.

My initial goal with this book was for me to learn more about myself, but I soon realized that there was so much more that could be of value to a greater audience than just one person. Why would I struggle to find answers, and then keep all my findings to myself when it could be of value to other people?

In this book, I will explain more about how I did this, and how you can follow in my footsteps to find answers to the questions you carry on your shoulders. Learn more about yourself, find out why you work the way you do, why you make the decisions you make, and how you can do even better in the future by knowing about specific and unique functions and abilities that you possess.

But books should be interesting, educating, surprising, inspiring, and also have a clear path or the so-called "thin red line" to follow. Preferably, also have a structure that makes the chapters blend together in a good way.

Just like in the winter, when the raindrops falling from the sky turn to snow, and every snowflake forms in a unique shape, I wanted to do something unique; something that could be easier to digest and to make use of. I decided to write this book in a way that fits me best and not how it's expected to be done. I wrote everything that came up in my mind and then I picked out the parts that I thought would be of interest to you as a reader.

In addition to contemplating, I have always been working on preparing myself for my next challenge every day by reading topic-related books that I find interesting. I have also enjoyed and often been inspired by the various talks on the well-known site TED.com and even ended up performing on the TEDx stage multiple times with my own TEDx talks.

If you would like to see them, just go over to www.KarlLillrud.com and subscribe to the news feed to know about where I speak next and to see the recorded presentations.

[GLUE:] First vs Last impression

As the first exercise of this book, I want you to do the following. Look at this picture and try to write a bullet list of 5-10 points that describe the person in the image.

Write down the first thought that comes to your mind and don't overdo it; just let your inner voice speak to you and write it down. Save this as a piece of paper inside the book or take a photo of what you just wrote down, as we will get back to it again later on in the book.

First section
Getting started

Write your own book

How I wrote this book

No limits

The structure

Write your own book:

Q: How can I share everything I have learned and inspire the world?

My thoughts around this:

When I started writing this book, I discussed this project with a friend of mine. After just a few words, however, he stopped me to say that he was going to work on writing a book himself and that there were a few things that I was talking about that might end up in his book as well. He wanted to make sure that as he would be writing about some similar stuff, I wouldn't later feel that he copied from my book.

I told him straight away that I would be honored to see my thoughts inspire and empower him. I truly hope that every one of you who is reading this book considers writing your own book. I will even help you get started on your own book by sharing my methods throughout the journey of this book.

We are not talking about publishing the book yet. That is something that comes later if you even feel that is something of interest to you. Instead, start by writing your questions and thoughts down and you will see how the things that you have been pondering upon for years start to structure and line up in order. You will be amazed as you find that your mind becomes less cluttered, and you start operating like a well-oiled engine.

[GLUE:]

First, try to find some questions that you may have kept to yourself or questions that you may not have even asked yourself yet without focusing on the answers. Give it a try. Start by thinking about one thing.

Let's start with a couple of easy examples:

1. *How can you find more inspiration?*
- *Change your route home from work to have other impressions in your everyday life?*

2. *What are your comfort zones? What steps did you always want to take but were afraid to do so?*
- *Quit your job to do what you've always dreamt of doing?*
- *Start your own business?*
- *Figure out what makes you different from other people?*
- *Learn to do something that you never thought of doing?*

3. *What put you in the position you are in today?*
- *What were the circumstances you have faced and how did you choose to deal with them?*

4. *What made you evolve from being a child to the person you are today?*
- *Was it your family, your friends, the area you grew up in, the way you lived your life, or something totally different?*

5. *What decisions have you made that have had the greatest impact on how your life evolved, and why did you make those decisions?*
- *How have the choices shaped the real you?*

The questions I talk about in this stage are about you and your own life. Once you get started, you will notice how easily things start flowing like a river from inside your mind.

And you will soon notice that you start feeling a sense of relaxation as you answer your own questions.

"Think about it, the answers are within you."

-Karl Lillrud

You will soon see the benefits of doing this exercise just like I did.

How I wrote this book:

After doing the above exercise, you should be able to appreciate what I meant by the previous paragraphs. Assuming it will be as much of a pleasurable experience for you as it was for me, I cannot wait to share more of these practices with you as you go through this book. To start with that, let me tell you about how I wrote this book.

A couple of years back, to be precise when I was 19 years old, I learned about a software called MindManager by Mindjet. This was the first time I came across a software that let me write down my thoughts in a floating structure, just the way they floated in my mind. It was perfect for my needs, and my way of working to structure my ideas; and I learned that this way of creating structures is called mind-mapping.

Mindjet.com and mindmeister.com are both very handy in creating mind maps, and if you start using any of the two, you will find that they can be of help in many situations. It's just up to you to find out how you can make the best use of it.

No limits.

For this book, I chose to work with mind maps as it was easy for me to drag-and-drop the different paragraphs and ideas to build up the structure I was looking for, and I built up the chapters in a way that I felt gave the best result. In the end, that's how the red line appeared.

I can then move through the book just like I move through my thoughts. It's like a world map, or actually, more like a star chart which connects chapters (galaxies) and moving columns (planets) between the chapters so that you can visually see the entire book as a painting, and not as a document.

The structure:

I see the chapters as layers, one layer upon another which will eventually create something, that is incredibly strong, *the new you!* To make the chapter you read even stronger, I have put in some exercises. To paint an image in your mind, I call them the "glue" that makes the layers stick together to build what will become a solid structure for you to take with you every day as a helping hand in the many situations of life. You have already come across two of these exercises in the previous pages.

The glue is meant to slow you down, stop for a moment, and make you think about what you just read so that your mind can convert it from a thought to a memory that fits into your situation.

I talk more about the method to make better use of your mind in my second TEDx talk that you can find on my website. The glue is also there to make you question different areas on your own.

I personally have been going on a similar journey as you are about to embark on while reading other books that include tips and exercises like this one. When I am listening to the audio version of a book, I'm normally driving or doing some other task and my hands are occupied with other things and hence, it's not suitable to do these exercises. So, I pretend that I will do it later, but I know all too well that that's not going to happen. And thus, I miss out on some of the goodies in the books, and more importantly I fail to convert the thought to a memory, making it less likely that I can make use of what I learned in the situations when I need it the most.

I believe that if you try to do some of the "glue" exercises you will find them invaluable. I do hope that you find the time to do these exercises and engage yourself better.

[GLUE:]

Learn one new thing every day.

At the end of your day, as you go to sleep, say out loud, "Today I learned..."

At first, the people you live with might look at you a little funny, but you will see that they too will follow in this exercise soon enough. I came up with this idea years ago to make sure I was learning something new every day.

After you are done with school or college, it's not really in your mindset to focus on learning new things each day. Your day is full of all the things you have to do, making you forget about the things you learn along the road. You don't get the time to cherish this new knowledge. But by doing this easy exercise you will earn the feeling of success each day, and that's the feeling that pushes you to new heights.

I assure you that you will actually feel younger and happier after just one week.

If you find it complicated then contact me, and I will personally coach you to get started on doing this before you go to sleep every day.

As you do this, you will end your day with a feeling of success and your subconscious mind will prepare you to reach even higher set goals for tomorrow.

"Today I learned..."

SECOND SECTION

My early years

Outside-the-box thinking

By practicing you get better

Outside-the-box thinking:

Q: Why and how did I choose a path different from the people around me?

To be able to "think-outside-the-box", it's important to know what the "box" is. I call it the regulations or the fence that holds us back. The box is the walls made up of all the things we have been told over the years, about how things are, or how you are supposed to perform or not perform a task. Simply put, the box is whatever limits us from doing something that is not supposed to be done.

If you follow the regulations, the probability is high that you get no further than what they allow and you will never reach further, or get there faster or become more successful than the regulations allow you to. Because you lack a competitive edge.

My thoughts around this:

For me, the walls have been the challenges I've had to face because of my dyslexia. I had been going to school for about 8 years before I got help with my dyslexia, and at an early age, I discovered that I did not come to the same conclusions as everyone else in my class. The way teachers tried to teach me was simply not fit for me.

To learn by just listening was difficult or close to stupidity, and when someone told me how something is supposed to be, it wasn't as easy for me to digest and accept what the teacher said, unlike my classmates.

For me, it was easier to learn by actually understanding it, the so-called "learning by doing" and in the end, I not only had a deeper understanding of the topic itself but also about the things surrounding that topic. This made me understand the entire space and the dependencies of how things are connected together, instead of just limiting my understanding based on what I was taught by the teachers. My success did not come from confining me with rules that prevented me from under-standing the full width and more importantly held me back from thinking outside the box.

"Restrictions dull your competitive edge."

We are all given choices in school. It might not be as clear to us, but in principle, it's to choose right or left.

I did not choose right nor left, I chose my own way.

To some extent, it has also been about proving to myself that it's possible; that what people said was impossible is actually achievable, and that the given path or the regulated path is not the only method to reach the desired result.

I have just like most other people, grown up with people I looked up to, like my father and my grandfathers. All of them were successful within their area of profession. But the difference between them and me was that they were "intelligent", and I had learned in school that I obviously was not "intelligent" as I could not gather "knowledge" like the people around me.

When I was a kid, my (mis)perception of "intelligence" was that if you could memorize things like the other kids and get good scores or grades, you were intelligent. This included things they taught in school like how many kings Sweden has had, and when they died. I, to this day, have no idea about when a single king was born or when they died.

As a child with a limited way of explaining things to myself, I used one of the easiest ways to explain this disability to myself. I thought of myself as "stupid", because I could not memorize these kinds of things in the same way as the kids around me could.

But I could take in loads of knowledge in ways and areas that were relevant to me, things that I found logical and things that interested and inspired me. Then and only then, when I found a meaning to carry that knowledge with me in my mind, the doors opened to record it in my mental library.

It did surprise me, however, that I had so much difficulty taking in the other kinds of knowledge. Often, I received low scores in the tests in schools, and I was on the "bad" side at almost

21

all of the times when we got grades or test results. And we all know that "bad" is the opposite of "good" and for a kid, good and bad can be very easily translated into smart vs. stupid.

As I was not given or taught the tools that fit my way of thinking and operating, you can imagine what that did to my self-esteem as a child.

As I've been writing this book, I have been searching a lot inside myself and going through the memories of my life, and I found one more source of my way of thinking.

As a child, my father taught me the importance of understanding the rules of any game. This understanding has formed and shaped me in so many areas that I can't even understand it myself. The more you understand the rules, the better you become at outsmarting your opponents. Understanding the depths and limits will also let you take detours with relatively less risk, giving you a superior edge.

I was part of the Scouts as a kid, and there I could apply this understanding. We competed a lot against other teams; it was always a game but with great interest to win. It was then that I truly learned to find loopholes in rules that would give me an advantage.

From time to time there were competitions where the rules were written in a way that was meant for us to interpret to find other possibilities, which is also one source of my alternative way of thinking. I understood that rules are intentionally either written to keep us away from specific paths or to direct us on a given path or perhaps try to help us by showing us the currently known best path to follow.

The problem, however, is that it is the "currently best-known path", and as time goes by, everything slowly changes but the rules stay the same.

I have much to thank my father for but if I were asked to pick out only one of the best tools in my toolbox, it's the ability to dare to look where others don't, and to read between the lines.

"As time goes by, things evolve but the rules stay the same..."

By practicing you get better:

Q: How can I improve myself?

My thoughts around this:

As a child struggling with schooling and trying to understand how I needed to process information for myself, I felt a need to improve myself. I started on this quest with small things, but before I knew it, I was trying to improve myself in anything that I did. I would think about what the conventional method to do a task is, and would often try to find an alternative way of doing it which would let me reach the goal faster or more efficiently.

We have all heard it before, but it is true in so many ways. By doing things that you don't feel is within your comfort zone, or perhaps even things you fear doing, you evolve. While it is natural for people to fear the unknown, challenging yourself will help you to improve yourself and to get to know more about yourself. You will also learn how to adapt according to the situation and, more importantly, evolve.

It's in these situations that you will get the most out of life.

Example: Let's say that you live your life in the exact same pattern every day.

Taking the same bus to work, talking to the same colleagues every day, eating the same type of food in the lunchroom every day, watching the same type of TV programs every day, going to sleep at the same time, and then waking up at the same time in the morning just to repeat the process one more time. What new impressions, what inspiration, and what new answers did you find in this (perhaps) exaggerated ordinary life?

My goal is to share how I changed my way of working, from accepting to questioning things, even the things that might have already been answered or proven by me or someone else before. There are so many things I have been taught that can be done in a specific way but I realized that more often than not, there are multiple ways to achieve that same goal. That one way of doing something, that we know of today does not have to be the best way. As time passes and things change, it seems logical that doing things the same way over and over is wrong. The path most threaded is not necessarily the only one, or even the best path to the destination; it's just the most widely used because people tend to be comfortable with familiarity, instead of doing something different which might prove to be more difficult even though you were trying to make it less difficult.

With the tools and experience available to us, we can almost always do things smarter, better, and more efficiently. This opens up new possibilities and discoveries and we may even find hidden solutions to our existing problems.

Second Example: Let me give you another example that most people can probably relate to. Many years ago, you learned how to tie your shoelaces. You probably believe that after doing it thousands of times throughout your life, you can do it faster and perfectly.

But what you learned back then was never questioned, as you were a child listening to every person that taught you one thing after another, like in this example about how to tie your shoelaces.

If I told you that there is a way to do it both faster and better, would you do it?

I am confident that you know how to tie your shoe laces and you were taught how to as a child.

This is the faster and stronger way that I have learned.

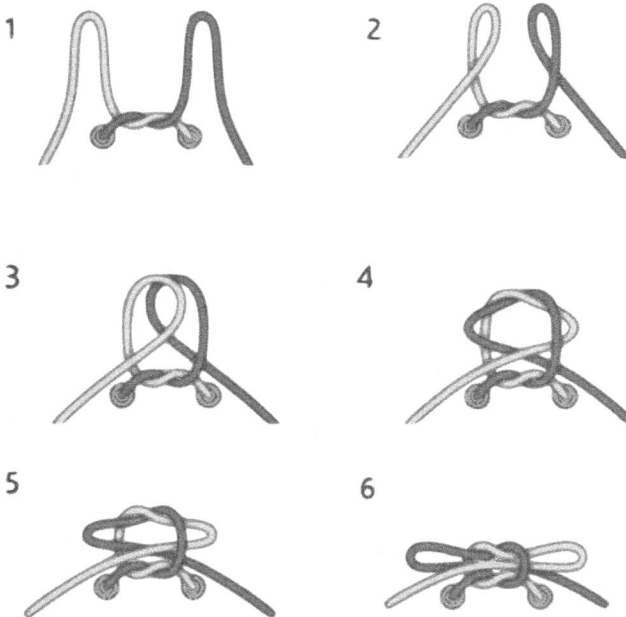

This new and improved way of tying your shoes that will save you time, the knot will look more perfect and keep that knot in place better, straighter, and stronger.

Go to www.KarlLillrud.com to see a video where I explain the exact steps so that you can take this first step and start improving yourself by learning how to improve the way you tie your shoes.

"The path most treaded is not necessarily the only one, or even the best path."

Third section:
Knowing and Improving Yourself

Happiness Coupons

The impossible history

Thinking outside the box

Outsourcing, creating a team and other alternative solutions

Do what I do best

How to manage your thoughts

Knowing how to distinguish facts from false information

Happiness Coupons:

Q: Why do I not treat money as sacred like other people?

My thoughts around this:

I have, just like most people, been working at companies, and with tasks that I did not find to be interesting or fun all the time; basically doing tasks that were then just a job that had to be done.

At that time I had no monetary issues. Although I had a good salary, that was not all. I had a plan for money management that helped me maintain a status where I did not have to worry about money. I knew how to structure my spending according to what was available, and that ensured that I did not have to worry about money at any point.

Example: Since I had seen many people in this society start focusing on gathering wealth, and in the process slowly develop a tunnel-vision for richness, I decided to view this whole system from a different perspective. I started calling money 'happiness coupons', and at that time it suited me very well.

Let me explain the way it worked for me, and there was a lot of thought process involved in it. It was not just a new type of currency but a new way of looking at money.

This connects to my belief that we need to inspire our children to find new possibilities everywhere, instead of always showing them the way. Explain to them the concept that some people might be willing to pay for chores that you find easy but which they find difficult or that they simply don't like to do. Then make up a price and discuss the price with the client to learn about proper pricing.

When that is in place, also consider teaching them the concept of repeat customers and subscription models. If you do this right, they will soon realize that they are not just selling a solution or a product at a price acceptable for the customers and for them, but also that they are selling their time. This will make them learn at an early age about the value of time, and how to make the best use of the limited time we have to spend on this planet.

When I went to work, I gave up some of my "time". You can see it as I sold some of my time to the employer at a price that was reasonable for me. I gave up an 'x' amount of time, and in return, I was rewarded with coupons (money) which I call happiness coupons.

Without these coupons, I would not feel as happy, as I could then not afford to have a home, buy food or clothes. So, as I saw it, I had two options.

I could give up large amounts of my time or a large amount of my work capacity (as some jobs pay more for more challenging tasks) and get rewarded with large amounts of these coupons that I could potentially change into a greater amount of happiness later.

Or I could give up less of my time and get rewarded with fewer happiness coupons, and be able to change those few coupons to something that would give me a smaller amount of happiness.

Do not get me wrong, I strongly believe that life is not all about money, but we also have to learn to value our time appropriately. Otherwise, it becomes difficult to understand how much reward we should be expecting for a specific amount of time that we've put into the work.

Identify what you want and then realize what you need to do to get there.

"Don't teach about impossibilities, inspire to find new possibilities"

[GLUE:]

Keeping in mind the lifestyle you want for yourself, try to calculate how much money you need for yourself and try to list the things you need money for, then sort that list in decreasing priority order.

Obviously, if you have a family or partner with a shared economy you have to write a more extensive list.

Example: Here are the top areas where happiness coupons are required:

- Housing
- Transportation
- Food
- Health (Gym and other activities)
- Insurances
- Retirement savings
- Fun stuff
- Vacation
- Monthly savings

= Coupons out.

Now write down how much one workday is worth for you.

= Coupons in.

Let's assume that a work month consists of 22 workdays.

22 * Coupons in ≥ Coupons out. (This should ideally be the result.)

Did your calculation sum up as expected?

In the previous chapters, we talked about how small changes to many things can lead to a greater impact. Now, apply the method you have learned to make changes in various parts of your life that can move you little by little towards your goal. You will see that if you follow through with these small changes, it can bring about a huge change in your life. The goal of this exercise is not to make you insecure about your finances in any way, but rather, to make yourself aware of your requirements and to prepare for them in advance.

"Identify what you want, and then realize what you need to do to get there."

The impossible history

I was invited to France to do a TEDx talk on the topic "Impossible".

I was flattered but knew that I had so much to share on this topic as I have been doing the impossible over and over again throughout my life.

As I was preparing, I did some research and found out that the word "impossible" was actually used for the first time in history in France where I was to be speaking.

It was used back in the 1400s, and has since then been translated into most languages to explain a thing that can't be done, right?

No, not really; according to me anyway. As I see it, it explains, not something that can't be done, but rather something that the person using the word doesn't know how to do.

Let's look at an example:

If I were to walk up to Buzz Aldrin and say that it's impossible to walk on the moon, he would reply that it's not at all impossible.

If I were to ask you if it is impossible to swim in frozen water for 20 minutes you would probably say that it's impossible; yet I know for a fact that it's not, as I have been doing it for years. Now when you know that, consider it the next time you hear someone use the word 'impossible' and really think twice before you use it on your own. Also, try not to use the word impossible when conversing with children. They need to keep their inspiration and learn on their own where their limitations lie and not be put down by us grown-ups.

As a person who loves challenges, I will tell you how I go about trying to make the impossible possible.

[GLUE:]

After considering a goal, let's say we break it down into 100 different elements. All of the 100 elements might not be solvable just yet, but let's say that 95 of the 100 elements are solvable. Probably more than 50 are actually easily solved. When you look at the 95 elements, you'll probably see ~5 that on second thought, you don't even need to solve right now to start working towards the goal.

Instead of focusing on the 5 that you don't know how to solve yet, you simply make sure that you solve all of the ~90 that you can solve. When that is done, let's have a second look at those 5 that were left.

As you are working on doing those 90 tasks, you will probably realize that you could cut some corners and choose not to do some of them yet.

Now when you have done 90 of the tasks, take a look again at the tasks left. Do you still need to do all of the 5 tasks that were set aside earlier?

Things have probably changed, and you might find that a couple of those tasks are not needed any longer.

About the necessary ones, review them one by one and split them into smaller parts. Let's say that each one of them can be split into 10 tasks. You now have 50 tasks again. Repeat the same exercise, again, with these 50 this time. Again, you will find a couple of tasks that you actually don't think you need to do any longer. At first, you had 5 impossible elements, but now you have 50 of which I am 100% sure that there are many that you now know how to solve. Especially as you have new insight from solving the 90 previous tasks.

By following this method, you will have your impossible task done in almost no time.

In some cases, it could be tough to break some of the elements down to 10 new parts, so in those cases, ask a different question. What else can produce the same result as this one element is delivering or in what another way can you reach a similar result?

Do that over and over again until you finally have no elements to solve. You have now done the impossible and now possess a great comprehensive understanding.

Congratulations! You now know how to do the so-called "impossible".

"I go about trying to make the impossible possible."

Thinking outside the box:

Q: How can I challenge my comfort zone and learn new things every day?

My thoughts around this:

This is for some people who are trying to have their first experience with stepping outside their comfort zone, and here is a short list to get you started:

1. *The first advice and the easiest one is to start moving, moving in any direction but the one you have always been moving in. Try something different. Even if it sets you off track for a moment, it's good, because you start to interrupt your old pattern and get new views which will lead to the new doors opening.*
2. *Go to Pub cons and meetups.*
3. *Start your own network and or discussion group and invite people you know. Have them invite people you don't know, that they believe will be of value to the group based on its theme or agenda.*
4. *Get office space in an open floor-plan office hotel, where there are many small companies in the same area or people of the same age as you are. You will both share your knowledge which will be of help to others and learn from them.*
5. *Reach out to people that you think could be like-minded, maybe offer them lunch and just see where it might lead. Be sure to explain why you are doing so, so that they misunderstand your intentions, and know that it could be of mutual value to them.*
6. *Do something for yourself. Stick your neck out, I promise you, you will not get knocked down. You might not find what you are looking for directly, but you will feel better as you continue your quest rather than then if you never did it in the beginning.*

Example: This is how I challenged myself to break out of my comfort zone and trained to swim in a condition where the air is -23 degrees Celsius and the water is only 2 degrees Celsius.

Years of experience with ice-swimming has given me an incredible amount of endurance strength and a deeper understanding of my body. Ice-swimming is a very popular practice in Sweden where people often run from the sauna to a hole in a frozen lake for a quick dip.

As both saunas and ice holes are the extreme opposites of each other, one extremely hot, and the other extremely cold, it makes sense to take turns into both of them to maintain a balance. It's challenging to stay in ice-cold water for more than a few seconds, and to stay more than 10-30 minutes is considered "impossible", especially if you were to do it without warming up in the sauna first.

Start by defining the goal, consider something that is considered impossible or unrealistic, just because it's so much more fun when you eventually reach that "impossible" goal.

First, I break down the elements and focus on the ones that I can do.

1. *I can swim.*
2. *I can learn how to swim faster*
3. *I can learn how to swim more energy-efficiently.*

Now I move on to the things that might be a little complicated and focus on how I can make those tasks easier.

To swim 500 meters in 2-celsius warm water is both mentally and physically difficult. But to swim 100 meters is not at all as difficult. So, by splitting the task up in 100-meter laps instead of one 500-meter lap it becomes mentally less complicated.

So, I set up goals with milestones along the way.

Now to the impossible things:

- *I can't swim when it's too cold.*

Analyze why. This does not mean that you start thinking about all the things that people have told you why it's considered to be impossible. Think about things you know for a fact, not rumors and assumptions.

1. *Fingers and toes freeze faster than my arms and legs because they are smaller and thinner.*
2. *When the water circulates around these smaller parts and I lose my body temperature faster than in the rest of my body, the blood gets colder and to protect my heart, my body decreases circulation in these areas and eventually shuts down circulation in fingers and toes which could lead to some severe damages or even amputation.*

Let's review these two statements.

I have a clear idea about the challenges and to overcome this, I must identify a workaround, a solution, or an alternative.

The problem is related to the circulation of water close to the skin which lowers the temperature faster in the areas that have a smaller mass.

Some alternatives are:

- Decrease or stop the circulation of water close to these areas somehow.
- Increasing the mass to make the body keep the heat.
- Increase my body fat
- Apply fat externally on my body before swimming

The solution I chose was to use neoprene gloves and socks which would hinder the close water circulation around my fingers and toes and this proved to be an effective enough solution to the problem without changing the entire setup since I wanted to do it with as little help as possible. Simply wearing a diving suit or even a dry suit might have made it easier but that would ultimately defeat the purpose.

Let's now look at another example using the same procedure.

Example: We have a goal. Buy a new X.

We all know the most logical approach is to find a store that sells X.

Let's say X is a specific type of candy.

Start by going through the obvious answers to where this candy can be bought. Or to simply put it, if the candy store is closed and opens tomorrow, where would you be able to get it earlier?

Think about what you would do if the obvious solution was not possible.

What are some alternative sources that could have that candy you want or a similar one?

1. *The grocery store*
2. *The pharmacy*
3. *The supermarket*
4. *The gasoline station*
5. *A friend*
6. *A neighbor*
7. *The Cinema*

Now try to think wider and be more creative. For the sake of this exercise, let's go as wild as we can, regardless of the feasibility.

8. *Ask your friends on social media platforms*
9. *Ask people you don't know in public groups on social media*
10. *Get a cone or a megaphone and talk out loud on the street where you live*

11. *The tax-free at the airport*
12. *Going to another country where they have stores that are open 24/7*
13. *The factory that produces the candy (they might do the production during the night, so it might be open if you have this problem in the middle of the night)*
14. *Calling the people on the board of the company as they often list the board members on the brand website.*

The list is long and you just have to be creative. You just have to understand how important it actually is to solve this particular problem and how much effort you're willing to put in to solve it.

Outsourcing, creating a team, and other alternative solutions:

All the ideas above were about how you could solve the problem, but sometimes you don't need to solve the problem on your own.

At times, I might not have the proper knowledge to complete a task or the time to acquire the knowledge to do it myself. So instead of learning how to do it by myself, I may simply outsource the work and pay someone to do this for me, so that I can focus on the key questions that I do want to put my time into.

You could also split the task into multiple pieces and work with a team. Or you could simply broadcast the task to a lot of people and have various parties working on it at the same time; which can reduce delivery times drastically and provide you with multiple options to choose from. (This very much depends on what the task is, and how easy it is to give instructions to the people you work with as it could also lead to a massive workload for you.)

[GLUE:]

Many people are not used to outsourcing tasks so let's cover some basics in this glue exercise. Obviously, there are loads of things to learn about how to do this efficiently, but that is too much content to cover here. If you feel this is something that really interests you, I would be happy to help you more, and if I get requests for detailed guides on this topic, I will consider writing a book on this topic as well. So, feel free to reach out to me.

First of all, you need to know what you are looking for. Let's consider the following situation as an example.

Example: Let's say that you have planned a vacation to Greece. But don't know where you'd like to go specifically since you are not well informed about the geographies of Greece. If you start googling about it you will find tons of articles about it, but you might want to know from the people in Greece.

If you state a simple question on a site like www.Quora.com, you can invite people from the platform based on their occupation and where they live, and they might happily share their knowledge for free.

If we take this to the next level, the actual journey there could be something that would need some extensive research. You might want to hire someone to help you with finding the best flight route and best ticket prices for you; and this could be easily done by recruiting a virtual assistant on sites like Fiverr.com, where the price for doing such a task starts from 5 USD.

You might also want a guide that takes care of you throughout the journey, which again could require some research, but you could find such people on the freelance platforms as well.

The prices for these tasks are normally much lower than you would expect. By outsourcing, you can save much of your time and also get to know some really good people with far more insight on the subject you want help with.

The freelance sites are divided into two parts; the freelancer profiles where you can search for freelancers and contact them directly, and the job posting board where you can post your requirements and freelancers can then bid on your project.

After you have set everything up on your side, you can post a request of what kind of work you want to be done, like for this example, you can post a request for a tour guide in Greece. Then you can filter so that you invite people only living in Greece, or set that as a requirement in the post. As you receive bids on your post, chat with them to make sure they can do what you need them to do and to settle on the terms and then select the person you think would be best for your job.

If you hire a person in a low-cost country like, for example, India, you probably only have to pay 1/10th of what you would do if you were to hire someone living in one of the capital cities in Europe. This, of course, requires that you change the way you work. You need to understand the difficulties and needs of offshore outsourcing. But the low cost can, in some situations, be the difference between success and failure; as when you are starting up a new venture, the funding is normally limited and you need to make the best use of every nickel and dime.

Other than the economic benefits, it is not only about your success, but also a success for the person you chose to hire if you do it right. Working with a remote company is going to be an invaluable experience for both parties but apart from the experience, there may be even more far-reaching benefits. Let me give you just one example, in the case of working with India, you can provide an opportunity to someone to develop above their caste barriers which may otherwise prove to be difficult for them when they work locally.

For those who do not know about it, the caste system is a Hindu system of retaining the occupation of the family that you were born into. This has been a barrier for many people to overcome, as it was widely practiced across the nation. As a result, people born into poor families had to continue working in minimal-paying manual labor jobs that their parents had been doing previously.

The caste system has been forbidden in India since 1949, but you can still see its influences in the rural areas of India. But in India, not all of them are Hindus; there are many other religions as well. For example, there are about 300 million Christians, which comes as a surprise to most westerners, including me, until I started to read more about the country to understand their culture.

This helped me a lot when I was starting to work with outsourced projects and team members in India.

Since then I have always read up as much as I could about a country and its etiquette when I work with offshore resources, freelancers, and companies in other countries.

Do what I do best

Q: Should I try to do everything myself? Is there a better way to do it?

My thoughts around this:

The obvious answer is no, you should not do everything on your own. But in some situations, it might be difficult or impossible to find any other way. I have been in situations where it all started with me working alone, and I had to take care of it all on my own. But the problem was that I did not realize when it went from a required temporary solution to something that was holding me back.

Example: Something I learned from running one of my previous companies is that I should not try to do everything myself. I am simply not the best at everything.

If I do what I do best, I will make more money that, I can use to hire people who are best at doing the things that I'm not good at. Which in turn, will make the company grow faster and save time for me.

But more importantly, I will have a more fun workday as I don't need to indulge myself in tasks that are not inspiring, challenging, and educating for me. By hiring more resources, they will, in turn, generate more money for me to use in other areas, and the total result will make the company or product more solid and allow it to grow faster.

[GLUE]: Do what you love doing

This exercise is about finding out what you love doing. You might think that you already know what you like doing and what you don't. To clarify, let us proceed with the exercise.

Listing the things you don't like doing is often easier so let's start with that.

Example:

Things I don't like doing are:

- Accounting
- Wasting time
- Repeating myself
- Delays due to poor preparations
- Maintenance

Things I do enjoy doing are:

- Challenging myself (stepping outside my comfort zone)
- Building things
- Improving things
- Talking to/ Sharing experiences with people
- Sharing my experience to inspire others

By going through this we see a clear pattern; one that can be used to know when to say yes and when to say no. This will help you figure out the tasks that you should start handing over to other people or outsource to online services. More and more things can be automated nowadays and if you don't know how to do it yourself, you could simply ask a freelancer to research the alternatives for you.

*"Do what you do best.
Get someone else to
do the rest!"*

How to manage your thoughts

Q: In what ways have my pedantic ideas during my teenage years helped me, and in what ways have they caused problems for me?

My thought around this:

Today this has evolved into not only my interest in gathering multiple "truths" or alternative solutions but to also focus on the full picture. As a result of that, I have gathered massive amounts of information which led to the need for proper structure in a chaos-pool of data. Let me tell you how I rearrange things into a well-defined structured mass, like the star chart I told you about earlier.

Example: As you join a new team for a new job or just happen to attend a new meeting, there could be an overwhelming amount of new information that is hard to navigate through. Especially because people might share the things they come to think of that could be of value to you in an unstructured way. In such cases, I have found mindmaps to be far more useful in collecting information and storing them with a proper structure.

Try to use the mind mapping technique, where you start with one level of threads, write down names, systems, goals, challenges, offices, teams, and so on. If you do this, you will see that the names could be put into groups, teams, and offices, which in turn, can be connected to a larger system of relevant and similar such groups. "Challenges" could be the focus areas for the groups; they could be something that you divide over multiple groups or something that you have multiple people from different groups working on together. As you do this, you will soon see that the pattern is there right in front of you without any heavy work. Try it out, as that's the best way to make it work in your favor and see how it happens before your eyes.

There might also be information that you have not found a place for, things which you could put in a mental note section or a topic called unstructured perhaps. Those are the details that your mind has pointed out for you to keep track of, which you will soon find useful in some other situations where that information becomes something of great value.

Mapping is a great graphical tool to handle these kinds of things, but after using it actively for a long time I got to the point where I needed a second layer or a second dimension rather. A dimension for things that are hard to handle on something that is just flat on the screen.

[GLUE]: How to mindmap scattered information

As you already know, I used mind mapping to write this book. But apart from that, I use mind mapping for so many things every day of my life. To give you an example of how I do this personally, let's take a simple example that many can relate to.

Example: Your partner calls you, and wants you to buy groceries on the way home from work. He or she starts listing everything they need hoping that you will remember all of them, but this is a task that many of us find difficult to do.

What I do is that I type all items down one-by-one in a mindmap; no structure, just one item per topic, and I call the mindmap "shopping list".

Then I think about the store. Let's say that the store has organized its sections with fruits, vegetables, meat, baking stuff, dairy products, soft drinks, and snacks in this specific order.

There may be some other sections like fish, candy, cleaning products, and so on as well. But right now, those areas are of less importance to me, and I can simply add them later if I find the need for them instead of starting out with a mindmap with unnecessary information.

Your mindmap is how you visualize things, not how someone else would have structured it.

So, I create the nodes:

- ❖ Fruits
- ❖ Vegetables
- ❖ Meat
- ❖ Baking stuff
- ❖ Dairy products

❖ Soft drinks and snacks

Now I start moving all the items I was asked to buy over the phone into these topics and now I can avoid having to run back and forth in the grocery store because of an unstructured shopping list.

Let me take one more example that we slightly covered above.

Example: You start a new job. It's the first day and you have 6 one-hour meetings where people from this new organization will get you on board by sharing information with you.

As a person who likes to have structured data ready at hand, I like to take note of any important topics discussed in meetings. At times, however, you might have much more information at hand that you truly have the need for. In such times, I use mindmaps to sort out the information which I have no use for and define the rest to a proper structure.

I name the mindmap by date and time and copy the meeting topic from my calendar. By doing so, I can easily get back to the information just by looking at my calendar as a reference.

Let's say, at the meeting everyone introduces themselves. I note down the names including some identifying features (like dark hair, tall, beard, etc.) to further improve the picture of the people in the room.

Some might say which team they are from and some might not mention the team, so I either ask what team they are from or just keep on taking notes.

I already have a two-layer structure, with team names and team members.

Let's say they then start talking about system names. They might give some more information about some of the systems.

I note down all of the points that are of importance to me or might be of importance in the future.

I then step into the other meetings, repeat the procedure with another file after introducing myself and saying that I will be taking notes.

I collect the information and after the meeting, I use the information I noted down to create two mindmaps.

1. Systems
2. Organization

In systems, I copy all the information from the meetings and with all the information I gathered from the meetings, I now have a rather clear image of the system and their purposes, requirements, and dependencies.

In the organization's mindmap, I sort the names of the people I have met according to their teams, ranks, distinguishing features, etc.

Collecting and structuring information at the same time is a lot more difficult than it may seem, but if you can manage to do it, you might be able to save yourself a lot of time.

With this example, I strongly encourage you to do this with any meetings you may have if you feel comfortable.

You can also use mindmaps for other things, such as:

1. Places you want to travel to.
2. A bucket list (things you like to do during your lifetime).
3. Your wedding plans.
4. Family finance.
5. Business ideas.

Knowing how to distinguish facts from false information

Q: With massive amounts of information, there can be conflicting information, duplication, and errors. How can I make sure I don't work based on rumors or false information?

My thoughts around this:

As you use mind mapping more and more, you can easily get to the point where you want to combine several mindmaps and interconnect details in them to each other. When at that point, you can start using several layers in the mindmap and may also start to feel the need for filters to make it easier to read.

Google is working on something called the "knowledge graph", which they claimed during the presentation was the new way of searching for the truth. They believe that this would help people look for factually correct information from the pool of widely conflicting information that is the web as we know right now.

As things are right now, anyone can start a web page and write whatever they like, for example, "Barack Obama is White and from Canada", and it might not be accounted for as being the truth.

You can now easily see the problem of handling massive amounts of information that might be conflicting. Almost like our brain which gathers information about each and every topic for us and then uses it as a thesaurus or encyclopedia to explain each and every situation back to us based on our previously known knowledge of recorded information and experiences.

Let's just put one more layer of conflicting information here to further explain the complexity, as there might very well be another Barack Obama in Canada, just not the Barack Obama that we think of first.

In their presentation of the new product, they have a three-dimensional star-map to visualize how information is connected to each other, which is like a mindmap but in 3D; and it's actively moving and evolving its knowledge about each item adding information as it finds out more on each topic and connects with other related topics and dependencies but also collect pieces of information that are wrong, assumptions and misunderstandings on the topic like for example when you use Google and get the list of potential long-tail searches. Like if I were to search for a movie star, it will show what most other people have been searching for with that movie star's name. If I make a spelling error, it knows about previously made errors to the spelling and suggests what the correct spelling is and asks me if I like to search for that instead, or it may even show the corrected search result without even asking.

There are tons of advantages to using mindmaps instead of classic documents or spreadsheets with tabs or any other ways of documentation, which might be an entirely new book in the future.

As this is a topic I believe in very much, I had to share a little about it to inspire you and make you think about the structure of your thoughts and how you document unstructured information given to you. I could not just jump past this topic and instead, I touched it just a little bit to inspire and show how this is a tool that enables you to find your own alternative solutions.

But enough about that and let's move onto our journey.

Fourth section:

Interacting with People

People are lethargic by nature

Constantly evolving

Feedback and its powers

Know your trigger points

How I do my work

Impressions

Flood your mind with information

Elevator pitch

Men vs. Women as entrepreneurs

Family and friends

Passing on my knowledge and experiences

People are lethargic by nature

Q: How can I improve myself to overcome other people's limitations, mistakes, and inability to deliver on every requirement of mine?

My thoughts around this:

If you are expecting some kind of delivery on a task or job, avoid being dependent on a single deliverer. These kinds of situations may lead to a single point of failure. Spread out the risk and try to think ahead to find potential pain-points and blockers so that you can solve or outmaneuver them.

I often run several questions or tasks in parallel with outsourced team members placed all over the world. Depending on the task, I often try to have at least two people working on the same task without them knowing about each other, as I've learned that the result they bring will complement each other, making the two deliveries combined at least 20% stronger than if I were just to do it with one person.

Or if it's about speed, I would have two people working on delivering what's needed as fast as possible. In some situations, to increase pressure on the team members, I might set up a "finder's fee" kind of payment scheme; instead of paying both of the team members I agree with them that the first one who delivers will get the full payment, and the other still gets half the price. If they chose to accept, I know that they will work even harder on making sure they deliver fast and with the best quality.

I also tend to try out different tracks of the same task to figure out what the best approach is. It's like reinventing the wheel, there might be an obvious path but I often want to see where that other not-so-obvious path might lead.

One can certainly find that this is taking longer as I need to identify the different tracks and then put them to work. But it also means that I can:

1. Reach the goal faster.
2. Learn more about the topic.
3. Will find alternative solutions.
4. Always act more creatively.
5. Not necessarily accept it as it is.
6. Think and process every little thing, or just step back and let the "ant-hill" do their work.

[GLUE:]

This is a method that I have used in so many situations, but the one situation that most people will remember is the one where we managed to do open water swimming even when the water was frozen to ice.

I have also done this when I had complex tasks to solve, like when I built my very first eCommerce engine from scratch or when I had a timeframe to launch a system that we had to build in less time than what would normally be possible.

Instead of focusing on the full picture, I made breakouts. This is something that today is called the lean methodology and Scrum agile process framework. It's used by all leading organizations today and has made a huge difference in the world of rapidly growing companies solving complex problems and even solving things that were considered impossible before.

Let's try to break it down in small but logical steps as a teaser to get you interested enough to try it out, and then when you see how powerful it is, you can find more information about it. Basically, let's have a Lean approach to it.

The old way of doing anything that required some sort of planning, processes, and structure was the so-called waterfall model.

What we should not start with, is to get blinded by the huge goal or the massive project or the limited-time plan or budget.

Instead, we focus on what we know and what we can handle.

If the team can't deliver what you need, go through what they can deliver, use this as a motivator, and a fact. The team has abilities and strengths that might not be seen as you don't ask the right questions.

Now as you have understood what they can deliver and why I'm confident that there are some parts that they have pointed out to you that can't be delivered and also commented on why.

Their understanding of what it is that is needed is most probably limited to what you have shared with them. They think and believe that you expect exactly what you defined when in reality, you probably want something different but couldn't properly get your expectations across.

Example: Let me give you a philosophical over-the-top example.

I stand in front of my team and tell them our project goal. I want to travel to Mars.

The team answers without a flinch that they can't make that happen.

So, I further explain my requirements.

I want my DNA to travel to Mars

The team starts to move and twist and start to think about how they could do this and rather soon realize that it should not be a problem at all.

2.9 billion base pairs of the haploid human genome correspond to a maximum of about 725 megabytes of data since every base pair can be coded by 2 bits.

To further try to improve our current situation each individual's genomes vary by less than 1% from each other, they can be lossless-compressed to roughly 4 megabytes.

To create a transport device to carry 4 MB of data to Mars seems like a much easier project than to transport my body to Mars.

And if we take it even one more step, how about sending one (or a bunch of) radio receiver(s) to Mars, and just transfer the 4 MB haploid human genome by radio wave. In the time it takes for us to transfer the radio waves, we may even have come up with further improved compression algorithms.

In every situation, you can revisit the statement and redefine it, or separate it in multiple smaller statements and specifications.

This keeps your team focused on the goal, without distractions or worries about the larger picture.

At the same time, you can involve other teams or do further-more research to prepare for the next sequence in your domino game.

Depending on how critical the project is, I have from time to time engaged multiple teams to solve the same task as I might know that not all will be able to solve it in time.

But even if all of them solve it in time, I can combine the multiple solutions into one and by cherry-picking the best parts from the solutions, I can create one combined super solution.

"I want to travel to Mars."

Constantly evolving

Q: Why do I get held up in thought when there is something I don't know?

I do this all the time; I get to a point where I kind of zoom out because there is something that someone said or a thought that I had, that caused a question in my mind about something that I did not know or understand yet.

My thoughts around this:

Like the examples before where we broke down a complex task into many smaller parts, let's follow the same approach but this time, we focus on the things that I don't know.

Every time I come across something that I don't know enough about, I look it up. It does not have to be something extravagant. It could be a word that I don't know the full meaning of, or what colors the flag of a country has, or the tax system in Greece, or how to purchase a house in Spain, etc. I have set my mind to the idea that questions are to be asked and that I need to find the answer.

By configuring my mindset to be looking for answers rather than accepting that it's just a world full of unanswered questions, I believe that I live a life like a quest and focus on evolving myself, as finding the questions to even the smallest question is a way of evolving. My entire mindset has naturally changed from the "normal" (to ask but not expect answers to all questions) to the improved version of me where I search until I find one or multiple answers.

I have evolved a mental process and procedure to do this.

For the trivial stuff, it's obvious. I Google the question and analyze multiple sources to search for the best answer, or in

66

some situations, multiple answers as there might be multiple correct answers to the question (like the example with Barack Obama and how Google treats information).

As you have already learned in the previous chapter, there are many ways of outsourcing tasks and you could do the same with finding answers to questions.

If you have a simple question, you can use sites like www. Quora.com. I use it daily to ask trivial questions that I then leave there and check back every now and then, as the question can be answered multiple times by multiple people.

You can invite people from the platform based on their occupation and where they live, and they might happily share their knowledge for free.

For the larger questions, I outsource the search for answers using platforms like Odesk.com, Freelancer.com, Fiverr.com, PeoplePerHour.com, etc. And often one answer is not enough, so I always search for multiple answers to the same question by giving the research task to several freelancers.

"Configure your mindset to look for answers instead of accepting everything."

Feedback and its powers

Q: How can I get some quick feedback and indications to understand if I'm moving in the right direction or not?

My thoughts around this:

You must talk to people about your ideas large and small, even the non-realistic ones, the funny ones, and all the other ones. Just empty your mind and have them tell you what they think about it. It is then important that the people you do this with are the "right" people; people that normally could be thought of as experienced, like-minded and positive so that you don't get set back or made to push the brake by people that only focus on the problems and worry about the risks too much.

Your family is often not the best audience for this as they are too supportive or their care for you may cause them to have biased views.

I did not find it that easy to find these types of personalities as I searched for them for many years, but I am telling you that you will succeed much faster and greater if you can get this type of elaborate playground for your ideas and thoughts.

A good mentor can be of great value to you I believe, which is why I both have a mentor but also work as a mentor. I have seen the great power of this and how it helped me succeed in so many ways. Since a mentor is a person that probably has done some of the things, or similar things for that matter, as you are doing, they can share their experience and guide you along the way so that you don't fall into loop-backs and get stuck at problems that they have experienced before.

"Birds of a feather flock together."

With people having similar minds and energies, amazing things can happen. The saying "birds of a feather flock together" is a saying that carries a huge amount of truth. When you are trying your best to be productive, being near similar such people can boost your productivity many-fold.

But in the workplace, and especially in entrepreneurial life, it's not as easy to find people with similar goals and values as when we were kids. That is why it is so important to find a group of similar people with whom you can stay connected and not only improve productivity but improve yourself as well. Focus on the people that bring energy and find a way to let go of the rest.

If you have lots of people around you, some will be good for you and some will be bad. It's important to understand which ones are good for you and why, and in turn focus on the ones that give you positive energy.

Feedback is of great importance but you need to know how, when, and why to give feedback.

If a person does not understand that it is the feedback that you are giving them or don't know what feedback actually is, they might or probably will see it as criticism, and then you lose the entire purpose of giving feedback and probably will receive a negative result.

It is therefore important to talk to the person firsthand to see that the person knows what feedback is and how it is used to help people evolve.

At that point start by removing your own "shield" and ask the person to always reciprocate whenever he or she feels the need to give feedback to you and others.

Then ask the person if he or she is prepared to receive feedback as in some situations it is not suitable to receive feedback.

71

For example, if he or she is stressed due to some problems at work or home or when the person has not had the time to have lunch or lack of sleep and so on. Always make sure that there is no one around that might make him or her uncomfortable or embarrassed.

There is much more about feedback to learn than this short chapter but what I mean with this is to open your eyes and get comfortable with using feedback as a self-improvement tool. You should consider asking for feedback to see how powerful it is in terms of self-improvement.

I have been asking for feedback about this book from the people around me. I asked for feedback from others so that I get a broader view about how people see this book, its values, and its weaknesses and areas that I should remove or elaborate more on.

Feedback is someone's opinion and depending on who it is that gives you the feedback and the type of feedback it is, you could take it with a pinch of salt or you might see it as something you need to learn from and change accordingly.

Know your trigger points

Q: At an earlier age, I often found myself in situations where I behaved as a porcupine; and by this, I mean that I could possess a quite thorny exterior towards a person. How can I deal with those situations better?

My thoughts around this:

I realized that this happened whenever I was told how to do a specific task in a specific way, which mentally put me back in school where I was told how to do things without being given enough information as to why I should do it that way and what I have to learn from it. I pondered as to why this happens and realized that I do not like being told to do a task in a specific way. Perhaps many of you feel the same way from time to time?

They can tell me what result they need, but I usually work best when I'm allowed to find my own way to reach the result, rather than have someone hand me every single step to follow like a machine.

I know that many feel the same about being given a manual, but what I propose is that you welcome this feeling and understand that this is your mind telling you to not follow the stream, but to do it your way. It might not always get done exactly the way it was intended and you might be standing there when you mounted that IKEA furniture with a bag of screws that you did not use, yet you know that every single one should be used according to the manual.

By knowing this about myself, I wrote this book as a guide trying to explain and give you examples so that you could use the ideas I share into a place that feels natural for you instead of simply following set instructions.

[GLUE:] Identify what you value

Take a pen and paper and write down a list of what you like doing separate from your work schedule; what your hobbies are, etc.

For example:

- *I like wine but at this time, have no interest in becoming an expert. I like the wine that I like and I don't bother to know why I like that particular grape, that country, or that blend or that vineyard. I decided to occupy my mind with other things.*
- *I love extreme sports/adrenaline sports. But nowadays, as I have a daughter and family, I don't feel I can sacrifice my overall health as I need to be there "protecting them". It's a decision that I have made myself and not a condition I have been put into.*
- *I loved our dog Monaco who gave me energy, love, and time to process some of my thoughts in another type of way during our walks.*

Know why you like some things and don't like other things, as this will lead you to understand yourself better regarding what makes you become a porcupine and what makes you become the best version of you.

Identify your trigger points and write down three answers to the following bullets.

What makes you:

1. *Relaxed*
2. *Stressed*
3. *Happy*
4. *Sad*
5. *Angry*
6. *Focused*
7. *Productive*
8. *Not productive*
9. *Inspired*
10. *Energized*

How I do my work

Q: Why do I want to know about the personality of someone first and then think about their roles or titles?

My thoughts around this:

As a child, I learned that all of us are different. As a member of the scouts in Sweden, I learned things I never learned in school. But more importantly, I could see with my own eyes how everyone from my school, that were part of different groups, the cool kids, the bullied kids, the silent ones, the cute girl and so on, did not have to fall in line as you needed in school and follow the teacher's instructions.

I learned that the silent kid knew birds and other animals by their names in Swedish and in Latin, the bullied kid was super strong and could lift up heavy things, the cool kid was fast as lightning and the cute girl had amazing writing skills. As a team, we could solve any problem as we were a mix of different tools.

At that time, I think my main strength was that I loved to chop up wood and was good with fire and ropes.

The value of our different key strengths is something that school never managed to show me and I'm extremely happy and fortunate to have experienced that, as it changed the outcome of my life.

There are many ways to build efficient teams, about which I can go on and on about, but I like to explain the values with one example, the "Escape Room". If you do it right, explain the concept before to the team members, that it's about everyone focusing on their strength and step outside their comfort zone. Afterward, analyze the outcome within the teams to make sure you get the most out of it.

Escape rooms are something that can be found in metropolitan cities almost all over the world and are much appreciated by companies to have as team-building activities. The employees work together to solve the room's riddles and mysteries.

This exercise helps the team members bond and learn about each other's strengths and abilities that might not be as easy to express in the workplace where everyone has a role and specific deliverables it helps everyone to get a chance to see each member's contribution. When working with others, think about what your mutual benefits are. What you can do for others, and what others can do for you. Since all of us possess certain qualities but not all of them.

[GLUE:]

To know about other people's key strengths and their limitations, you must be willing to learn about them in detail. It goes without saying but you will never learn if you don't ask.

As you learn to ask, you soon begin to understand how to ask the right questions and when.

When you go through tasks in a group, see how people react, see who stands out, and who tries to stay silent. Talk to them in person, rather than in the group, and ask about how they feel about the tasks.

Ask what they really like and why to widen the scope and ask why they do what they do and what they wanted to become as a child. Ask what they would like to do if they were dreaming out loud.

Ask them what they want to do in 1 or 5 or 10 years. You could even ask them about their hobbies, and how come they have these hobbies; what is it they enjoy with the hobby and why.

For example, someone might say Netflix is their hobby, at first it might sound strange but if you ask the simple question, why? The answer could be something like that he or she is interested in how they empower new actors that have no Hollywood track record, or how they use their platform to influence people and guide their thinking and their view of the world, or perhaps because it's the only time they have when the entire family is gathered together.

Open their pandora's box with them to help them evolve, and you will see how they will paint a map with you and show you things that you would never get to see if you did not ask.

They will often find trust in you, and you now have a person that will support you just as you support him or her, just by showing that you are interested in for real.

*"You will never learn
if you don't ask."*

Impressions

At an impressive weekend training, I did a couple of years ago, I came up with something new to me. This helped me learn a lot about how people see me and what people think about me.

We have already done this in the first glue exercise but to extend the exercise, this is what you should do:

For this to work, it is best to consider someone, or even a group of people, that you have acquainted with a short while ago (just a few days or maybe even a few hours ago). It can be done with people you have known for a longer time as well, but the time you made the first impression on them might have already faded out of their memories.

Ask the person, or even better, ask a bunch of people, one by one, about their first impression of you. If you do this at the end of a course or any other type of new group activity that you joined, they might all have the same information about you to base their first impression on. For example, your posture, your clothes, how you speak, what you say, and what they hear, as what you say is not always what people hear; they will combine your words with how you present yourself. Or they might believe that you have an underlying goal and will base their first impression on assumption and very few facts.

As you are doing this, you should explain to the person you are talking to, that you are doing this as an experiment to understand more about how people see you and then, after getting to know you what they have changed in their way of looking at you and their assumptions about you.

Write down what they say to the question, "What are your first impressions of me in no less than 10 words or bullets but not more than 100 words." It's meant to be the essence of their feelings, and you want to bring out the first thing that pops up in their mind.

Now, at a later point, ask the other question, "Please tell me about your current impression of me. Is it the same as before or has it changed after you've learned more about me?"

Go through the answers and see what most people answered. Do you like the first impression they have of you? Can you do something to make it more positive? Or what other things can you learn about yourself from this simple test?

Do you remember the exercise you did from the first chapter, in which I asked you to write your opinions based on the photo of myself? This is the same formula, but this time you will be implementing this from your perspective for your retrospection.

Flood your mind with information

Q: Why do I remember some things and other things are much more difficult for me to remember?

My thoughts around this:

By asking multiple questions, even when I understood from the first answer I was given, I got a deeper understanding of not only the topic in question but also the areas surrounding it.

But don't flood your mind with things that you don't care about, or things you can find out in an easy enough way, like phone numbers. It's probably better to have phone numbers in your phone than have them occupy brain capacity in your mind. Even if you have an endless capacity to memorize things, recording them into your brain requires energy which you might want to spend on more important things.

You learn how to learn new things, as you learn new things. I try to take in a massive amount of information every day.

I process information from about 5-15 Ted talks and 2-4 business literature books per week, just as an example of how much good information I digest, and this is not even counting all the other "standard" information from my daily work, the startup initiatives I'm involved in or my everyday life.

I have realized that a book that I found interesting can be almost as interesting, and sometimes even more interesting when I read it again just 6-12 months later. This is because I have evolved and now find other parts of the book of interest or understand what the author was trying to say.

"Don't flood your mind with things that you don't care about."

Elevator pitch

Q: How can I present my accomplishment without people thinking that I'm bragging about myself?

My thoughts around this:

This is something that I have always found rather difficult, to be honest.

You can't just go on telling people your achievements as for many, it might be considered bragging. But people who have similar accomplishments will understand that it's not bragging but rather a presentation of who you are and what obstacles you have overcome.

If you meet a new person, you have to analyze what kind of person they are to know what kind of stories they might be interested in.

Now if you analyze it right and do believe that you have a fellow entrepreneur in front of you or beside you at the table, you might present them with your accomplishments to gain traction and set up potential respect amongst you in the future.

In case, however, the people around you are not at the same level, it might come out as you bragging or being a charlatan, even. You see, this can actually become a real problem if you don't handle it right.

So, to make the best out of such situations, I looked around and came across a solution.

For those of you who have not heard or do not know of an elevator pitch, here is a summary.

The idea behind an elevator pitch is that you have about 20-30 seconds to say whatever you want to make an impression of you on the other person. Basically, like talking to someone on an elevator until either of you reaches the destination. It does take practice, but if done right, can leave a lasting impression.

Keep in mind that your elevator pitch should excite you first. After all, if you don't get excited about what you're saying, neither will your audience. People may not remember everything that you say, but they will likely remember your enthusiasm.

You need to identify the keywords. These are words of extra importance.

Impress without bragging. Make them feel that it is of mutual benefit to get in touch and that you'd like to have them in your professional network.

Practice your pitch, record it, listen to it, change it, and do it all again, until you feel it's good enough.

Now go to a friend and test it and ask for their opinion on it. Don't settle for a - "it's good". You need to know what specific parts they remember and what other parts they don't remember.

Did they get it right? What did they not remember and is it of great importance that they do remember it?

Remember to tailor your elevator pitch for different audiences, if necessary. Keep it in short sentences as it's easier to follow and remember a short sentence than a longer one.

Speak out, speak with a higher volume than you normally would do; not only to make sure the person hears you but to also stand out in the form of energy, and show the energy and power to the person listening. Use your hands to emphasize your feelings.

Pause between the sentences to make sure that the sentence is set. This also helps in maintaining the impression of a calm and goal-oriented person.

Finalize each sentence with a downward inflection. Follow your statements with confirmation that they are still on the subject and interested. If they are not able to follow, this will help you stand out as an authority on the subject better than if you just use your body language.

Don't speak too formally or in closed sentences. Remember that this is not a speech but a conversation. A one-sided talk tends to lose the interest of the other party quite easily.

Start with something that excites curiosity, a cliffhanger of sorts that increases the interest.

Talk with a smile and warm eye contact but be careful that you don't stare as that might make them uncomfortable. You could follow the example of news-readers as they constantly maintain eye contact without making it uncomfortable while also maintaining a smile through their entire monologue. Practice this as you will appear friendly and the listener will subconsciously register this in their memory.

Fine-tune your elevator pitch to keep it fresh.

When you get to know a new person well and can speak freely with them, ask them about what they remember from your pitch. You can gather unique insight if you can get their opinion on what they thought at the time and what parts from it they still remember. Remember the first and last impression exercise as this is based on the same principle.

Your USP (Unique Selling Proposition) should also be embedded in your speech.

Example: Hi. My name is Karl Lillrud. I have been an entrepreneur for 23 years and with my vast experience of starting up organizations as well as helping existing ones to grow faster and become more entrepreneurial, I started to work as a speaker and TED talk presenter. Nowadays I travel throughout the world as a speaker and mentor. All of this comes from my great interest in doing the impossible and inspiring people to do the same; about which you can learn more from my first TED Talk if you wish to do so.

Fine-tuned:

- Experienced
- Entrepreneur
- Speaker, Mentor, and TED-speaker
- End it with repetition, summary or call for action

After you have given your elevator pitch, ask a question that prompts a positive response.

"I would love to have lunch with you to discuss how we could interact and understand how I can help you reach your goals."

Here is a simple layout that you can use:

[Hi/Hello.

Your name.

Title & organization.

What you do.

Specify your goal.

What problems you solve.]

Do not tell them how you solve it. If they are interested, book a meeting where they can describe their issue so that you can provide a customer-based solution.

- Engage with a question
- Hand over your business card
- Connect with them on LinkedIn or other such sites and send a nice one-liner (ex: "Great to meet you just now and I look forward to that meeting").

Ask other people about their elevator pitch. Listen closely to what they say and how they say it. Make sure that the pitch is tailored for your audience.

*"Do not tell them
how you solve it."*

Men vs. Women as entrepreneurs

Q: Out of personal experience, I have seen that it's not as common to come across female entrepreneurs. Why is it so?

My thoughts around this:

I do not believe that this is because men are more creative than women. Rather, women tend to be more creative and do not necessarily follow the same rule-books as men, and thus they have their own ways of conducting business.

Our society often restrains us according to our gender and defines our roles for us. I believe this is a trait passed down all the way from the cavemen era. During that time, it was natural for the males and the females to be assigned different roles for providing for the family.

Men were supposed to go out hunting and procure resources to provide for all of the others in the family while the women stayed at home and took care of the children and did other similar chores. This trait can be seen even in a modern society where boys are encouraged to be adventurous and learn from their mistakes while girls are usually under close protection; they are very often restrained from being equally free and are not as encouraged to take risks.

This is why men grow up actively trying to push their boundaries, being creative and thinking outside-the-box while women learn to be more conscious and cautious of what happens in their vicinity. However, women under certain circumstances can show unnatural critical thinking and may come up with solutions that may not be visible to others when they sense a threat to their family or close ones. In such cases, they may take any measures to avert the danger as much as possible.

What I am trying to say is that they have the same potential for creative thinking as men and yet, because of societal reasons, they are often underestimated or restrained to boundaries. If you do not agree with me or have any other theories, I would love to hear your thoughts on this matter.

Q: How can we keep from making the same "mistakes" and instead treat our children equally without gender playing a role in it?

My thoughts around this:

In the case of our daughter Wilhelmina, I can say that I do not believe that I have been able to refrain from keeping her away from things that I could hurt her physically at first, but she would slowly learn more about her specific physical abilities and how to avoid things that cause pain.

I have, however, chosen to focus on the things that keep her evolving to build up a mindset based on my beliefs and pursue making things work not only the so-called intended way but also to find other paths.

Let me explain this more in detail in a glue exercise.

[GLUE:]

As a parent, we are the answer to all questions in our children's eyes.

Even before they can speak, we start explaining how they should do things both in words and by showing.

We will see how they get frustrated when they cannot do things the same way as we do them and so comes anger.

We want to keep our children from becoming upset both for them and for us to have a good everyday life.

So instead we do it for them, we help them with eating their food to cut the food, tie their shoelaces, eventually we think they are big enough to do these chores on their own and they start communicating verbally about why they can't do things and that they just give up.

It's the easiest trick to get us to do it for them as they have seen by experience from previous events.

I have struggled to inspire my daughter to find out how things are or how things can be done or even how we can find other ways to do it without looking at previous solutions.

When she comes to me with a question let's take a few different examples for you to train your mind and to have a quick response the next time this happens for you.

How does that work

1. Credit card

In my daily life, I mostly make payments using a credit card because of which, to my daughter, it was not obvious what money was and how much we had as we just swiped our card, and nowadays with the contactless payment options with phones and smartwatches the understanding for money and its value will be even more faded away as we don't have any contact with cash and not even with a wallet and a specific card when doing the payments.

Explain the value of money and the difference between currency and what inflation means to a currency

2. Clouds

As I was flying with our daughter, she asked me if we could take a walk on the clouds someday and I explained to her that we would fall right through them. Obviously, she replied, "Why?"

So, I explained the concept of water and how it goes through cycles which finally end with rain. But then she asked me how the drops can stay up and I could not answer her straight away.

The same night before we went to bed, we investigated the topic together and found out that every water drop that falls from the sky is a combination of 1 million vaporized micro water drops.

On a side note, she also learned how when the water evaporates from the sea, it doesn't carry any salt with it. She already knew that plants can't survive with too much salty water, so she was curious about seawater ruining plants when it rains down.

3. Production of cotton

Another day she asked me where clothes come from and the fabric they are made by.

Together we investigated the topic to find the answer, we looked at the full process from fields with cotton that are processed in the factories then made into a fabric which is then sent to the fashion factories where she also wanted to understand why a similar-looking T-shirt can be very expensive at a branded store and just as cheap at a local store.

How the label have created an attraction but also a sense of quality and style that they use when pricing the products but also that some use better material but some just chose to have a high price.

Together we go the full cycle to try to explain from the beginning to the end, to make sure she has good enough context and understanding about the topic to translate it in her mind to something usable for the future.

How do I do this?

This is one of my favorite topics. Today most people live a life where they feel they never have enough time. The answer to the question "how do I do…." might be "you do it like this" where you actually do it without explaining and going through the steps.

And I like to take it a few steps further.

When Wilhelmina started to request my help in doing things even before she started to talk, I did not show her how it's done.

Instead, I have always tried to show her how to figure things out on her own, pointing her in a direction but not showing her the way. When she gets stuck, I might just push her creativity by showing some perhaps stupid ways that you could do the same step to show her that there are many other ways. The examples I give might not give her the result she needs, but she now opens her eyes to alternatives and soon she figures it out on her own.

This builds her pride and believes in herself, it builds strength and not believe but know-how and power that whenever she is put in front of a problem where most other people would say they can't solve it she will twist it, mirror it, put it upside down and look at it from other angles trying to figure out the options as there is never just one way.

94

She is brought up with the mantra, nothing is impossible.

As a child, she likes to challenge me now and then, and the other day she had been thinking about one thing that according to her was impossible.

-Dad, if you are falling down into a volcano and a shark is chasing you, it's impossible for you to survive.

-In that situation, I would take the shark as it's dead without any water nearby and jump up on the back and surf on it over the lava to get out of the volcano.

See the thing is not about showing that it's always possible, but to show her that there are more sides to any story and any solution or problem and I just stipulated some additional facts which got me out of the situation without a scratch... right! In reality, I would have burned up before even getting close to the lava.

When you're asked, how you do that, I explain how, but also ask about what else we can do to reach the same goal or what other things we can make out of the tools and the building blocks we have. I believe that by making them think about alternative uses and alternative methods you train their creative mind to make it grow and improve their creative thinking.

Family and friends

Family and friends are really important and as you work more and more as an entrepreneur. You can easily lose touch with the people that truly care about you.

At that point, it's really important to identify how to manage time for personal, professional, and social life separately. Try not to overwork yourself. That being said, it is important to identify how much is too much according to yourself and your requirements.

Then calculate how many hours you want to work without losing touch with friends and family.

Identify and choose timings when not to work.

When I go to sleep, I always put my phone in flight mode. At first, I started with the 'do-not-disturb' mode but soon decided that I did not want my phone to have any reception whatsoever while I was sleeping. The world would not end, and any issue that might be critical would have to wait until I got up in the morning. This helped me improve my sleep, which in turn improved my productivity.

As when my phone was not on flight mode a small part of my brain was still staying active to handle any income message or call, perhaps not in a way that I was aware of, but still in a way that used some of my attention span and energy. I like to think of this phenomenon to be similar to a device in standby mode, it still does use some power but perhaps just a few percent compared to when it's being used.

When I go on vacation, I go through my email settings, and as I have several email accounts for different projects and customers, I choose to deactivate some mailboxes on my phone that I know can wait till I'm back. By doing so I filter the selected ones out. This helped me improve my vacation and I felt more relaxed when I got back to work again.

I have also used another simple yet effective method to separate work life and my personal life.

Instead of having one email app on my phone, I install one that I use for my own mailboxes and a separate email app for my work email. By doing so I can choose to deactivate push messages on the work mailbox and not get disturbed outside of office hours when I'm not being paid by the client to work.

Passing on my knowledge and experiences

Q: What can I do to help other people with struggles similar to the ones, I have worked within my past?

My thoughts around this:

For me, one of the most beautiful experiences is sharing my knowledge and thoughts with my daughter. But I also realize that it has a drawback of its own. I would not be who I am today if I hadn't learned all those things through experiment and experience. Thus, I struggle to reason if it's okay to just hand her down this knowledge rather than letting her discover on her own.

That is why I now try to push her towards the right direction without being too blunt on how to do it. A mistake many parents make is to give their children everything without any question and the children hardly have to struggle for anything on their own. Being able to trust your child to be able to stand up on their own after taking a fall is a very crucial quality as a parent.

A child who has not struggled much in his or her childhood for anything tends to have a hard time as they grow up; when they realize that they have to start doing things on their own, especially when they have to start looking for a job.

Instead of simply giving your child a weekly allowance as pocket-money or to cover for their weekly expenses, ask them to come with tasks that they feel they can do. This could be something like washing the dishes, dusting the house, doing laundry, etc. It's then up to them to present their idea to the parents and ask for an amount of money that they felt they deserved for the work. The parents can then accept or negotiate accordingly.

This incorporates what we talked about within the chapter about the happiness coupons but also includes so many more elements like creativity, knowing your worth, finding your own path.

It's almost like a startup with an idea (the product) that you are to sell to your target customer.

So instead of simply handing over money to them, you could teach them about not only the tasks they want to perform but also about money management and how employment works in the real world.

Fifth section:

Finding Your Inner Flow and Increasing Efficiency

Life outside the office

Habits can be a double-edged sword

Immortality

Collecting everything

Track your day and analyze how you use your time

Empty your mind

Forced relaxation

Health

Food and nutrition

Think about your goals and focus on them

Identify your natural spring

Q: Where do the ideas come from and how can I keep track of all of them?

My thoughts around this:

I realized that I'm some kind of idea machine, most probably because my mind stops focusing on the obstacles when I need it to be creative and I put myself into a problem-solving mode. I then operate in a sort of brainstorming gear where I just push forward with good and sometimes not so good ideas, but the goal at that time is to always be moving. Take step by step, some steps will actually make me move backward but when that happens, I learn so much more than if I would always be moving in the right direction and incomparably more than if I were to just standstill.

But the next challenge is that there are no assembly lines to constantly handle the things my mind produces. So, after a short while, it all gets piled up, and I realized that I needed to empty my mind every now and then.

I have been doing this with the mindmaps and I started a mind map called 'Ideas' where I write all of my ideas down. After a while and after several sorting and regrouping I felt the need for a filter function.

Due to the way I developed, and more or less forced, my mind to work, I got to know that not all ideas are to be used. I created a scorecard system for my ideas to fulfill the purpose of a filter.

"I created a scorecard system for my ideas"

[GLUE:] The Filter

The way that I have developed my filter is to note down all the pros and cons. A few criteria I have used are listed below.

- *How to make money?*
- *How to maintain?*
- *How to market?*
- *How much time I will get back?*
- *How close I am to a solution?*
- *Money to market*
- *How much money I will get back?*
- *The resources needed*
  - *How many?*
  - *What type?*
  - *Price*
- *How does it look with competitors?*
  - *Locally*
  - *Globally*
- *Gut feeling*
- *The appearance*

By writing down all your business ideas (Yes, all of them! And by following the steps in this book, I am confident that there will be many,) you will be able to go through the list or preferably a mind map and structure them once per year or as often as you find suitable. And as you structure the different ideas you will see what areas of business dominate your mind, and also find ideas that complement each other or fit well together and find new ideas that fill in the gaps.

As you learn to use this method, you train your mind to pick up the ideas and you start to process them, which will lead to more ideas day by day and help you fine-tune your senses.

You see, there are similarities to the previous topic that we have talked about which dealt with not asking questions or not pursuing the answers deep enough.

As you go through the list of ideas, you will see how some ideas make more sense when grouped together.

As an example, I might write some main topics like this and then group all the ideas accordingly.

1. Web-based services.
2. Physical products.
3. Business with employees.
4. Other.

By finding your natural spring of ideas you learn more about yourself regarding which ideas you could naturally deliver best.

As a consultant, I learned that how you dress affects how you are accepted by the people you work with. I learned this the hard way as I was working in one of my customer's offices, being dressed in a suit. I worked with people from many different segments of the organization, high and low in the hierarchy.

For the ones on the higher end of the hierarchy, it was just normal and to be expected to be dressed such. But in my role, I had to get work done in many different areas, so when I approached the teams down in the hierarchy, they did not respond as I needed. When I explained what was needed in their own language, they felt that it was really strange that I could go to such depths with the problem and actually help them solve the problems.

When I dressed down slightly and removed the suit, I was respected over the entire organization in a better way in general and could get more work done in less time as I fit in, in a better way.

When I had to give presentations for the steering committee for the CIO or something similar, however, I did dress up slightly again for that day. So, what I'm trying to illustrate is that it's important to read the environment, as small things like clothing and appearance can make a huge difference between failure and success.

Life outside the office

Q: What can I do with my spare time and how can I feel more happy?

My thoughts around this:

Every day when I came home, I was gladly welcomed by our dog Monaco.

Even if I were to be exhausted, I knew that I just had to let that go and focus on him for a while as we took our walk after work.

During that walk, I would also let go of some of the stress and frustration from the day's work as he asked for my interaction and to take part in the walk. It truly was a great time and did bring me both positive feelings, mental and physical relaxation.

Love for your work is a very important part. Not only because life is more fun if 8 hours of your time every week-day are spent on doing something you actually enjoy and feel that you get something out of, but also because if you love your work you will not care so much about those 8 hours. You will not feel that work is work, and instead, you will view it as something that provides you with both a challenge and satisfaction.

But a hobby is equally important. You should find something that relaxes your mind. Letting go of the focused thoughts on your business ventures might bring you a different type of happy feeling.

[GLUE:]

I was experimenting a couple of years ago with a friend of mine, Marcus Werme when I realized that I wanted to find a hobby or rather a way to enjoy exercising.

Both of us seemed to have the same urge and both being in on it easier to stick to a schedule of doing things outside our comfort zone as we pushed each other.

We started by writing a long list of sports that we wanted to try out.

1. Capoeira
2. Japanese jiu-jitsu
3. Karate
4. Thai boxing
5. Kickboxing
6. HipHop dance
7. Cross fit
8. Shooting with guns
9. Shooting with arrows
10. Pool
11. Dart
12. Crossbow

...and so, the list goes on. We had a much longer list of activities and prepared so that we knew where we could try these out and made sure we could have a test session as well as which days that we could join on. Basically, sent an email to all of them and the ones that replied with the information we needed were put up on the list. Every week we then just rolled the dice twice and went to do whatever the number pointed us to.

We then analyzed which activities suited us best by looking at things like.
• The time needed in total door to door

- Equipment needed
- Happiness score
- Price
- Availability
- What type of result will we get?
- How much time is needed until we get good at an activity

"Let go of your thoughts."

Habits can be a double-edged sword.

Habits can be good. For example, I have the habit of waking up early in the morning, which helps me clear my schedule by planning ahead in time. Habits help me work on auto-pilot mode when I have to follow a previously defined pattern and the outcome is an expected one. This is the time when I don't care much for outside-the box-thinking or being creative or smart.

But just like in the gym, when I do my workout, I do different routines all the time. And I do not focus on one thing (muscle), but instead, the things that surround that one thing (involvement of multiple muscles), which gives me an overall better workout that challenges my entire body and not just the larger muscles.

For instance, if I want to work-out focusing on my triceps, I do that by doing dips and Kettlebell lifts back over my head, standing on a Bosu balance plate. I do chins with the bar behind my neck and so on. As you can see, the goal is to balance the workout for the smaller muscles and the joints which form the triceps or the parts around it.

If I just did triceps workout with dumbbells, I would not gain the same result at all. This is because when I do different workouts every time my muscles never get into a habit. Always putting pressure in a slightly different way will make you see much greater results in a shorter time.

The brain works the same way. So, don't go to the same lunch restaurant every day. Don't say you can't when you can, just because it's easier to say that you can't do it. Push yourself.

There are times for habits and there are times for staying away from habits. Whenever you get into habits you will soon learn that there is nothing to learn from them, you are on auto-pilot and would you really like to live your life on auto-pilot when you can go out there and explore life?

Another example from my workouts. It's a strict law for me to work-out Monday, Wednesday, and Friday. Nothing can change that. Except for the things that can change it... I would never replace my workout schedule with anything, be it fun or work. I would figure out a way to get both done. But from time to time, there are things that you just can't plan for and when that happens you should not beat yourself up about it. Just take it with a pinch of salt and make the right decision, don't waste energy on frustrations.

As always know what to do and not do.

Some things must, should or will bring the best results from being habits or strict routines. You just have to learn when to make use of it and when not to.

"You don't learn from habits."

Identify alternatives to reach the same goal

This is somewhat similar to thinking outside-the-box. You know that when you are on a trip, there are almost always alternative roads to reach your goal on the map.

There might be a freeway and then often there is the "old road" that was the main road before the freeway was built, and then there might be a dirt road or simply a path that will lead you to your goal on the map by taking all the smaller roads. Most probably the freeway is built as straight as possible and offers higher speed but at the same time, you will get to see far less, and get fewer impressions.

But that is the smaller picture. You could instead of just going by the car that might be your natural way of transport, travel by train or airplane. Now to imagine it in an even bigger picture, you could go by hot air balloons in lines or even walk or swim. Instead of going in a straight line to reach that point on the map, you could draw that line in the opposite direction, and as the earth is round, the trip will be much longer but you would still reach the goal.

Or if you have to get to the point faster, you could reach out to hire or even buy a private airplane or helicopter. This could be done by contacting your bank or to present your idea to investors.

Do the math and see if it might be beneficial in the long run to invest a larger amount of money to reach the point faster or get your idea up and running faster. In many cases, you will see that it is possible that doing just that might give you a steep curve that should not be avoided.

You could run around but you could also just cross the field, which is the shortest way or you could even choose to go the opposite direction altogether.

Immortality

At an early age, I built up the belief that I was immortal. Yes, it might sound stupid but let me tell you the short story.

My grandfather, a well-educated man was a professor, a surgeon, a doctor, a fireman, a member of some secret society that he never talks about, an elite gymnast, a programmer, and an astrologer. The list goes on, and he is a man that has had a great impact on me and in my eyes, a person with a lot of knowledge that is of value. And when he used to say something, people listened.

He said that you should always buy the car with the strongest engine so that you could drive away from any dangers that might appear. He was used to crashing his car very often. Something that was never spoken about, and there was just a new car in the driveway.

He broke his neck two times, once in a car crash and once as a gymnast on the bar.

He often told me that he had a hard time in school but still, in the back of my head, I knew he had taken himself through so much and learned so much. He was left-handed but back then you were not allowed to be left-handed so he was forced to become right-handed, even though his entire body screamed and was telling him how wrong it was.

I did realize that he and I were different in that I could not to read and memorize things as he did. But I still knew that if I focused on the goal without worrying about the dangers and challenges along the way, I would reach it.

That does not mean that you should not be aware of the dangers, but instead, that you should train your subconscious to handle the part that might scare you or set you off-course, out of balance or make you lose your focus.

"Being immortal will make you more daring to take risks and therefore achieve more in life."

It's with the active part of your brain that you yourself control that you reach the results desired with the expected outcome.

Practice does not mean everything. In school, I learned that you should practice learning. But they did not teach what they meant by practice, or maybe they did not understand themselves what type of practice really made a person evolve.

By repeating already known knowledge you are just traversing down an already discovered route. But by learning bits and pieces of what's around the area of interest, you learn how, why, when, where, who, and so on. You can start discovering your own routes.

Example: Milk is tasty and white. That's a fact and you learn that at an early age. You then learn the standard things like where the milk comes from and how cows look. You may also have learned about pasteurization and how cows are milked. But dig a bit deeper. There is basically one female milking cow but there are many different kinds of milk on the store shelf and even if you stick to the one standard milk, it will taste different in summer compared to winter and so on. Why is that? Never stop asking yourself questions, by doing so you will always evolve and learn what's in the shadows, which will help you make better decisions.

Ps: Milk tastes different in the summer compared to winter as the cows start eating green fresh grass and stay out in the sun instead of indoors eating dry dead hay.

Collecting everything

Q: Why did I use to collect everything as a kid and how did that habit shape the future me?

My thoughts around this:

It started when I was a kid in kindergarten. I collected everything. I was a classic "sakletare" as it's called in Swedish, which means someone who searches for things to find.

I used to collect things that were of interest to me like sticks, stones, metal cords, and other such materials that I could use for craft. A stick, a rope, a rubber band, and a metal cord could be used to make something great like a slingshot.

Once I started growing up, I started collecting other things like matchboxes, coins, football cards, and so on.

I use this idea of collecting things every day, even today as I collect knowledge that I combine to build something even better. It is not who we are, but rather how we use and reuse the knowledge and experience we carry with us in different ways, that show what we can become.

Time and value

Q: How do I manage my time amongst the chaos of everyday life?

My thoughts around this:

My interest in optimizing the use of time started when I was a teenager, and instead of walking from the bus to my home, I was running to minimize the time spent on doing nothing productive. Layers on layers have now produced the "me" where I make use of all my dead time, the time that normally would not be used for anything at all or where you do one thing but could do two things at the same time.

That is how it all started when I realized I was hacking my time.

I also learned another important thing after a while of optimizing everything, I learned that 100% learning or making use of all time available for learning and evolving is not the perfect recipe for personal growth. You have to mix it with fiction and facts. I realized that my life, all of a sudden, was all about some kind of work, every thought in my mind was either related to work or how I could improve the work I was doing. I started to feel no interest in life and got some type of short depression as I did not see the value of anything any longer.

This made me realize that I had to rethink this and figure out how I could keep the focus on efficiency yet keep in touch with "real life" while keeping some time for leisure activities.

I started to try to relax by engaging in random activities. It could be watching the waves on the yeti at our country house or watching some really bad yet fun sci-fi.

"I hacked time."

[GLUE:] Know your time's worth

- *What is one day worth it for you?*
  - ➢ *In terms of money.*
  - ➢ *In terms of knowledge.*
  - ➢ *In terms of time.*
  - ➢ *For yourself.*
- *How many days are your own personal days?*
  - ➢ *Count and see how many it is per year.*
  - ➢ *Sum it up using your age and your expected lifetime pension and education and pre-education years.*
  - ➢ *How many days did you get?*
- *Now go back to step one and do it again with this result in mind. What do you want to change and what outcome will that give you?*

You see, you don't have that much time so do it right.

Okay, don't get scared and start backing down thinking you can't do what you want to do. You can! Just stay focused and I give to you these tips and tricks for you to keep with you.

Example: A steady long-term consultant contract could be of higher value than a high paid short-term contract. But not if:

- You have a bunch of short-term contracts lined up one after another with a higher hourly rate.
- You don't feel for the assignment.
- The commute will be a waste of too much of your most valuable asset or your time.
- You get no personal development or further experience that can be of use during this assignment.

Track your day and analyze how you use your time

Q: How do I stop losing time?

My thoughts around this:

Knowing how to utilize your time to the fullest can be a very useful asset to achieving your goals and acquiring success. To do that, let's run some numbers first.

Statistically speaking, a man in Sweden (as I'm from Sweden) lives for an average of 80 years and a woman for 84 years. To generalize, let's say, a person living in Sweden has an average lifespan of 82 years.

Let's assume that the first 15 and the last 10 years are not personally controlled productive time for the person. So, from 82 years, let's take away 25 years, so we are left with 57 years.

As a Swede, we have 5 weeks of vacation by law. During vacation, most people do not think about being productive or learning new stuff. The vacation is for the family as a whole. This sums up to 5.4 years of vacation during your 57-year work life.

We are now down to 51.6 years.

During each year we have 226 workdays that we subtract which give us 94 days per year that we have left to work with as our own time if every year is 365 days.

There are some celebrations like Easter and midsummer and also family events like birthdays and so, that does take away the entire weekend or days of the weekend. In general per year, I think we can take away as much as 25 days more, which leaves us with 69 days.

During a normal weekday, most of us wake up, get ready, and go straight to work. Other than work, many of us have other tasks as well, like picking up groceries or dropping off/picking up the kids to/from school. For the sake of our calculations, let's say we have 4 hours during the day when we are truly free to devote our time to what we want.

So, 69*4=276 hours is the total amount of time that you can use per year, which is only 11.5 days.

But we know it's not really true as you often have to make time for some unforeseen or unexpected event or task lest estimate that 20% of our time is taken up by these types of events, leaving you with actually productive time with somewhere around 248 hours.

You might enjoy watching the television during your free time, but to me, watching TV shows with advertisements every 10 minutes is unacceptable. Even if you learn something from the show, 15 minutes of ads every hour is still time stolen from you which you might rather put into use into something better or more productive.

If you watch only one hour of TV per day, every day of the year with 15 minutes of ads, that adds up to 3.8 full days that you waste just watching ads every year.

I hope this makes you think and realize that my running from the bus to my home was maybe not such a stupid idea as it sounded in the earlier part of this book.

Now that you know this, you have to do something about it. I have, and I can say that I have so much more time than just 10 days per year which I use to do the things that I love and choose to do.

"How do you spend your 10 days of free time per year?"

Empty your mind

Q: What do I do to declutter my mind?

My thoughts around this:

In an inspiring Ted talk, Daniel Tammet tells us about how he, as a person with Savant syndrome, thinks about mathematics. He, unlike most of us, sees numbers as colors and shapes, and when numbers are added or subtracted the colors and shape change naturally. For him, the shapes and colors create a feeling that can be expressed in painting.

I have not learned to calculate like Daniel but for me, mind maps are similar to that as they enable me to document a natural flow of my thoughts. This in turn takes a lot of stress off my mind.

As I have discussed with you before, cold water swimming happens to be a hobby of mine which also acts as a great stress reliever. When you disconnect your active mind while swimming, you are solely focusing on staying alive through your subconscious focus and your previously defined goals that your conscious mind focused on. This helps me detach myself from too many thoughts and helps me focus more on what's important.

In the last chapter, I have listed some more tools that I use to organize myself and declutter my mind. Some can be used to relieve stress, while some focus on your memory and speed up the input of information and such. Feel free to look up any of them online and learn more about how you can make the best use of them.

Forced relaxation

Q: What do I do when things get overwhelming and it is tough to calm down and relax?

My thoughts around this:

Relaxing your mind is not always about documenting your ideas, however. Sometimes I have too many things going on and I feel like my mind is flooded which might make me dizzy and unable to relax. During those times I can't even meditate and I need external help to get relaxed.

And I found the perfect tool for me. A bed of nails, which is great in so many ways but I will just mention some things and how it works.

The thought itself might be scary for some of you, and if you would lie down with your body weight on the tip of one nail only, it would penetrate your skin and hurt you severely. But if you lie on many nails that are mounted side by side without any separation, you suddenly get a fixed structure without air in between the nails. You can now realize that this is no problem at all and you could lie, stand and jump on it without hurting yourself, as it is just like walking on the floor in your house.

If you now take away every second nail there is a small gap but still possible to stand and jump on it without it hurting too much. It might feel a little bit more than before, however. Just keep taking away the number of nails that are suitable for you, and you will realize it is not at all impossible to lie down on a mat of nails.

Again, we have the impossible situation of standing on 1 nail but the possible solution of standing on 1000 nails.

In the mat of nails that I use, I have a rather large separation between the nails and when I lie down, I have to focus on this task and nothing else at first. I need to relax my muscles as tension makes it worse and my body forces my muscles to relax and by doing that my mind automatically flushes the active thoughts that were distracting me and making me stressed. This helps me focus on a single task. It is like some kind of automatic survival mode that is close to what I have experienced during my open water winter swimming as well.

If you don't like mindfulness exercises, meditation or yoga, or any of the other methods to get relaxed mentally then this is something you should look into.

But also if you enjoy all of these activities and feel that you are in great control of your mind and your body, the nail of mats will make you expand your understanding of your body and you will easily hack your body to be in better shape to have relaxed muscles and to work with self-healing from the inside.

Improve your focus

Q: As a dyslexic, I have always had a problem with focusing on tasks in school. What did I do to change that?

My thoughts around this:

For me focus is very much connected to building up or having an interest in a particular topic, the problem might be that you have multiple things that interest you. There are many ways to improve your ability to focus but I suggest that you find the things that keep you focused on a task, then see what you can do to increase that particular thing. Fine-tune it and work systematically. This is something that I have used a lot over the years and it has saved me both time and money.

Here follows some easy advice.

By blocking the senses that are not needed for this particular task, you will divert your energy and brainpower to the senses that are required and intensify them.

Example: When you enter a dark room from a light-filled surrounding, you usually get blinded and can't see well. So instead, close your eyes, and listen to what you can hear to create a feeling or even a view in your mind. You have your memory and the sounds, the smell and feel of the room, you hear how sound bounces and you can even feel the size of the room with your body. Trust your senses.

If you listen to an audiobook close your eyes. If you read a book, block your ears. Listen to classical instrumental music or just simply block out noise by using earplugs, if you want to really taste something close your eyes and try to block out sound so that you only open the taste and smell senses.

Another way to get you easily started is by working with music.

- By listening to binaural beats, you can fine-tune your focus.
- By listening to music that gets you energized you can increase your energy.
- By listening to music that inspires and/or empowers you, new paths are created in your mind and new solutions can be thought up.

Health

Hacking my destiny would not be possible if I don't take care of my health and my mental health is as important as physical health and by seeing a doctor once in a while you can get some answers about your body's condition.

Make sure you are okay by contacting a doctor you trust or who is recommended by someone you trust. Then go to a second doctor and ask for the same analysis to check if there is anything that requires any further analysis to get a better understanding of your current physical condition. Then pick up the first doctor's analysis and ask the second doctor for a second opinion. Make sure they understand you want to know what you can improve to get better, and not that you criticize them.

A yearly checkup makes sure you are as good as you can get, according to your doctor's tests.

Keep in mind that doctors in many countries normally don't include an investigation of your vitamins and minerals nor your mental health or stress levels. These require other types of tests and doctors.

I value sleep very highly and know how important it is for my mind and my body. I separate the two entities, where "me" is my thoughts, knowledge, experience, and my body are just a tool that I control to make sure I can get whatever I need and do physical things with.

I have elaborated with sleep to see what happens and how I am affected by too much, or too little, or no sleep at all.

I have also worked on making my sleep more efficient. It might sound crazy, but what I mean is that I worked on improving my sleep.

When I sleep, I focus on getting the best possible sleep so that I don't waste time in bed with low quality sleep.

The easiest thing to start with is to analyze your sleep quality. I started using an app called sleep tracker on my phone many years ago. It tracks my sleep pattern, shows a nice graph, and provides me with great statistics.

When I go to sleep, I input the type of day I had with checkboxes like:

- *Late supper*
- *Stressful day*
- *Workday or not*
- *Workout or not*
- *Early in bed*
  and so on...

After a while, I can go back to the days that stand out in which my sleep patterns have been better than the other days, and I can then see what I had done during those days to see what similarities there are between those days which I can use to improve my sleep so I can take the right action.

Food and nutrition

One time I was really frustrated because every day at around 15.30 to 16.30, I used to get so tired and I would almost fall asleep. After thinking about it a lot, I thought it was the result of poor nutrition. So, I started wondering and searching for solutions that could improve this situation. I spent a lot of time searching for the right combination of nutrition intake and a proper diet suitable for my body.

I believe that no diet plan is perfect and every person has a different kind of requirement. When I say that everyone has different kinds of requirements, I'm not talking about allergies or anything like that. What I mean is that the vitamins and minerals that your body requires are not the same as everyone else. It all depends on what kind of lifestyle you have, what work you do, what exercises you do, etc. Some fibers might be difficult for your stomach to process and some others could have effects on you which may not be considered allergies, but still give you a negative outcome.

So, I started with this many years ago and looked into what things made me better. The year I started this, I had serious problems with gastric ulcers.

I straight away started to eat the food that did not give me pain and stopped eating things that did give me pain. So, I stopped drinking coffee, orange juice, and eating fatty food like pizza or other fast food. I only focused on eating things that my stomach could easily digest.

One thing led to another and I now, every day, think about what food I eat and what energy I put into my body.

As an example, I try to not consume sugar, especially in the forms of soft-drinks or candies.

But I do think that sometimes it's okay to eat the "wrong" things as a treat, as long as I don't overdo it. Also, some vegetables are better than others, like:

1. *Broccoli*
2. *Carrots*
3. *Avocado*
4. *Ginger*
5. *Blueberries*
6. *Goji berries*

And the assortment that is classified as "superfood".

If you have not heard about 'superfood' you should look it up online and you will soon see the positive effects they bring to your body and how you can improve your health and energy level by just fine-tuning your selection of food. For example, did you know that broccoli contains almost double the amount of vitamin C per 100 grams compared to what you find in an orange? To be precise, average broccoli has about 89 grams of vitamin C while an average orange only has about 53 grams.

I normally only drink the following:

1. *Green tea*
2. *Water*
3. *Lemon water*
4. *Ginger drinks*
5. *Fresh fruit drinks*

And if I'm going for a soft drink, I prefer a kombucha which, with its the fermentation process has positive effects on your body.

Don't be a sucker for sugar. Avoid the ups and downs that the sugar rush gives you.

This is easily done by eating light every third hour. You don't need to eat an entire meal, but do keep fruit like a banana or so, to stop getting that tired feeling that you normally get during the afternoon as your blood sugar drops. At that point, it's easy to fall for your body's scream for energy and have something with sugar or caffeine.

80/20

If I eat 80% good, then I can eat 20% that's not as good.

To start with, don't consume soda during the week so that you can have soda during the weekend. Soon enough you will realize that you don't even need the soda during the weekend and that you actually feel better without it.

If I feel like having a soda, I think twice if I really want this or if I can have a cup of green tea or fresh fruit drink instead.

Think about your goals and focus on them

Q: Where do I want to live my life? Here, or somewhere else? What are my requirements and how can I get more out of life and the time I have in this world?

I have, for many years, had a goal to be able to work from wherever I like. By making that possible, I could be at the beach in Thailand for one week, in a hotel in Hong Kong the second, and traveling in Italy the third.

I do like to travel and it feeds me with new impressions and gives me mental energy and experience.

When I was living in Sweden, I was always looking for more. So, my wife and I had a goal to be on a vacation every 7th week. It doesn't have to be a long vacation, maybe just for 4-10 days.

But during these vacations, I always do some sort of work. I go through my ideas and try to see what gaps I can fill out in my mind-maps. I come up with new ideas and then work on it when I have the time.

I also get loads of energy that is of great use when I'm back, and I use that to deliver more and perform better at work after the vacation.

As we now moved from Sweden, Stockholm to Spain, Marbella we don't have the same desire to get away on these vacations as much, as we live a life where we get so much more out of every day that we don't get the urge to travel much anymore.

Learn to control your inner flow

I realized that I had like a river flowing through me. If I was standing on the side, I would see the water rush past but if something were to float by, I would just have to watch it pass and might not be able to catch it. So instead, I jump into the river and sometimes just float with the stream, and sometimes stand still to catch anything floating by and from time to time decide to walk up and sit on the side, to just relax about it all. I learned that just like with any river, swimming against the stream requires much more energy than swimming with the stream and I try to focus on finding the right time to jump in or potentially let something pass by if I feel that I'm too slow to realize what's floating by.

Finding your inner stream and learning to control it will become a crucial advantage to you in your everyday life. A few ways you can get started are:

1. Yoga.
2. Meditation.
3. Breathing techniques.
4. Writing down ideas (at the moment they happen, or they might never happen at all).

As your subconscious mind presents ideas to your conscious mind, the idea has not yet been recorded in your memories, it is not related to anything but just a thought without any connections floating around. That is why those thoughts come and go and as they are not a reflection of your conscious mind, it's difficult and often impossible to find the same thought again if you don't write it down directly. Turn this into a habit that we talk about in the idea mindmap. Find your way of recording it and you will be amazed about what your own mind is telling you after a while as you see the patterns of your thoughts and ideas.

Sixth section:
Think, Focus, Do

How fast is a thought?

The brain

Understand yourself and reflect on your past

Inspiration

To fail is not to fail...

The fisherman

Your personality

Bucket list

How fast is a thought?

Speed of thought is really the speed of minute electrical impulses in our nerves, which are formed via the changes in the concentrations of ions inside and outside nerve cells, which is roughly equivalent to 100 meters/sec (360 km per hour). The speed of light is 299,792,458 meters/sec (1,080,000,000 per hour). You can see that that light is approximately 3 million times faster than the speed of electrical impulses.

But as you know, if there is a car crash or any other major event, it feels like time is slowing down as there are so many focused thoughts and images passing by. Things that are from right there and then and also perhaps images from your memory bank. It's almost as if you start thinking at the speed of light. If you think about it, you might be traveling at, let's say 100 km/h and maybe the point of collision is 3 meters away, but the distance your thoughts have to travel is probably less than a centimeter, and that too, at a speed of 360 km/h. So yes, your mind will have plenty of time for processing the information and may present many things to you, at that seemingly long time that it takes for your car to travel those 3 meters, but to focus on the current situation all other thoughts are put aside so that you only focus on one thing and that is why it feels like time is slowing down. Because your mind is 100% focused on one task, imagine what you could do if you could control that way of working.

Do you realize that this means that we can "slow down" time? with mental focus?!

Know why you do the things you do and make the most out of it.

I always try to do at least two things at the same time to maximize the use of my time, which, I know, contradicts what I just told you about focus and slowing downtime with the use of brain focus power, but most of the time I do not need to have 100% focus at those tasks, tasks that you have done many times before or where you are in a relaxed state.

Example: I take my car to work. I do this due to various reasons:

1. I can't take my bike even though I want to, because I have a problem with my foot at the time of writing this chapter.
2. The parking outside our house is more expensive than me paying for the tolls and diesel fuel. And the parking is free outside my office and our car is an investment and not an expense.
3. I get to learn from the audiobooks and TED talks I listen to every day during this commute.
4. During the morning commute, I drop our daughter at school, which I would have a hard time with if I did not take the car. I do really want to be a part of her life even within these small obvious things like leaving her at the kinder-garden so that we get father-daughter time which is important to me and her, I'm sure.

Another example is why I ride my bicycle.

1. It is a splendid workout.
2. I get a rush of adrenaline, as I always compete against my own best lap time.
3. The transportation is at a very low cost. (The tires or other parts may require maintenance.)

Another example many of you may find relatable:

It's a mindset to be more and more efficient with the time you have at hand. For example, as I walk around in our home, I always keep an eye open for things that should be in the area that I'm heading. For instance, if I go to the kitchen, I look around for any utensils that someone may have forgotten to put away properly, or if I go towards our daughter's room, I look around to see if any toys are lying around. Basically, looking for things that I can take with me, that are supposed to be in the other room that I am going to or passing by.

But from another perspective, I incorporate this method in my work too, as I know that the work I do is connected to other people and somewhat relies on deliveries from them. That means that I, from time to time, can't run at the same speed all the way until I am done as I have to wait for other teams, or team members to deliver their part in the chain.

For example, for this book, I started writing it a long time ago and every now and then I would feel that I had no time or inspiration to write, so I stopped for a while. Instead, I started on some other tasks like the book cover or reading up on the different alternatives to getting it published. I talked to some people and hired some freelancers to do research for me or to work on the design of the cover and so on. They could then work for a while on their own and I could get back to the book with new energy and inspiration.

So, what I'm trying to say is that I don't believe in 100% mindfulness as that would lead me to be stuck every now and then waiting for others' deliveries.

"We can 'slow down' time with mental focus!"

The brain

For being such a small part of our body, surprisingly to most of us, the brain uses a huge amount of energy. Around 20% of our total energy expenditure happens in the brain.

To learn more about how your mind functions and handles information regularly I can suggest a book called "Your Brain at Work".

Different parts of your brain handle different types of information. When you process all new information, like when driving in a new country, the part of your brain called the 'prefrontal cortex' processes the information and this is where a lot of energy consumption takes place.

When you drive from home to work, however, which you might have done a couple of hundred times by now, there is no new significant information to take in, and thus the part of your brain that comes into play is called 'basal ganglia'. In contrast to the prefrontal cortex, the basal ganglia require very little energy and thus you could probably do it for 4-5 hours without getting tired. You may have noticed that on such drives, you usually just drive and take turns without even putting much thought into it as the repeated steps are hammered into your brain, almost like being on autopilot.

This is because your brain doesn't really save any of the information that is recorded by your eyes, as it compares with previously known information and learns that it already have that type of memory saved in your memory bank, duplication of data is something that is a challenging problem for us to solve with our computers while our mind seems to have found a model that rationalizes the data and save it based on its value and the update state after first comparing with the version it has saved earlier.

The fuel in your prefrontal cortex, glucose, and oxygen, is being consumed much faster than most people are aware of. Just try by taking a totally different way to work, a way you have not driven to work ever, and you will see that you will feel much different when you arrive and that your energy during the day will be affected.

But it's not just that you use up energy as new inspiration, a new impression, and new experiences somehow boost your energy levels also, just like taking a fresh breath of air.

Subconscious thinking is something I talk about over and over in this book and this is another great example.

The other day, when I was tired and went to bed, I fell asleep but my subconscious mind suddenly remembered that I had parked my car on a street that was supposed to be cleaned that night, and if I didn't move my car in 5 minutes, I'd get a fine. My subconscious mind had woken me up from sleep to have me correct my error.

I normally pay close attention to the street cleaning schedules as the fines are rather expensive, so when that happened, I was a bit frustrated with myself and tried to analyze the reason behind this error of mine.

I remembered I met one of our neighbors earlier that day, and we discussed the general parking terms on our street. He told me that they did not change the terms for parking so it was okay to park my car there. So, when I returned later that day, I had that thought in my mind when I parked my car but I had forgotten about the cleaning night. You see, normally it wouldn't have mattered but on a cleaning night, we're not supposed to keep our cars parked there.

What I'm getting at is that it was very obvious to me that my mind reprocessed all the information that I had from the day during my sleep, like checking for errors deeper in my mind. Once an error was found, it was not flagged as critical until just 5 minutes before the cleaning was to be started. Had I not woken up and corrected my mistake, I would have gotten a ticket.

As you now know about the speed of thought, we do know that we have some limited possibility to process information in terms of speed. But I am sure that you have had a moment where it seems like you anticipate what is about to happen and it soon happens before your eyes, and it's like time slows down. For everyone who has seen the movie Matrix, it's like bullet time, where you actually see the bullet from the gun and can dodge it. Now that type of slow-motion is probably not something you have experienced, but when you see the wine glass overflow or when you see the car in front of you doing something that might affect you in the form of an accident, you might remember being extra perceptive of your surroundings.

So, I gave this some thought today.

I am by no means an expert in the area, but I love to think about problems or situations just like this. About how this happens, why, what's the logic behind it, etc.

Let's use the example of what you might experience in the event of a car crash.

You see a car driving in your lane but there is something unusual in its movement.

Now your eyes see what happens and your brain starts to analyze this but instead of just accepting what's going on, it's like your brain freezes the time but actually, that's not what's happening.

I believe that the brain reprocesses the information given to it, now working with our full capacity. Instead of just using one part, the conscious uses all our senses and our entire brain is active, not only the small part that is normally active.

The different parts of the brain process the information in their own regard and then cross-reference with all the other parts. These layers then combine to give you the possibilities of what might happen and suggestions as to what you can do about it.

Now some people handle this situation better than others. Some just sit there and see the event take place, but other people do handle the event and try to make the best out of it.

These are the people that have been actively working in stressful conditions and in situations that require quick decisions with a large impact.

I believe that if you want to and actively work towards achieving more, you can do it, as opposed to if you think you can't, you probably won't.

I, for example, am working with the speed in my hands. I want to be able to pick up a glass that falls from the table before it drops to the floor.

Understand yourself and reflect on your past

Try not to over-stretch yourself to meet unrealistic expectations as you will have a very hard time reaching your goals of success. If you do reach it, it might have not been worth it compared to the effort and sacrifice you had to put in to get there.

By reflecting on what you have done, what you thought, what you prepared for, or whatever you like to reflect upon, you learn much more than expected. Do this as a habit and you will see how your subconscious has its way of helping you out with making things possible and delivering results.

This entire book is me reflecting on what I have done with my values and what I want to do.

Identify your defects and turn them to effects. Some of mine are:

1. Dyslexia

At first, this was disability, as I could not follow in school like other fellow students. The school also treated it as a disability, but once I started to learn more about me and this ability, I learned that I just did not operate in the same way, especially when it came to solving problems. I realized the many benefits this has given me and today I'm proud to be dyslectic.

2. I really do not like to have to say things twice

This only applies to my professional life. When I'm working, I might hand over a task to someone, and after that, I remove that task from my mental checklist. Thus, I don't touch the task until the person gets back to me with the result.

This could be seen as a disability to some as I don't follow up but to me, it's a way to put my focus into other areas where it's better utilized. I do tell people this in advance so that they know about my view of this and can avoid any problems caused by it.

But I also use this in the opposite direction, meaning that I try to take the burden off the shoulders of the people I work with whenever I feel I might be a better person to handle certain tasks.

This has also proven to be a way that might help some people perform even better, as they feel that I trust them and thus want to deliver on that trust.

3. Hate when things are late

This is related to the above and I keep a steady contact with the team to make sure that we don't lose time nor focus. If we lose time, I try to see what we can do to make up that time thinking outside the box.

In most situations where time is lost, it's due to some sort of distraction that was not planned for. These distractions are up to me as a leader to take care of so that my team can work as efficiently as possible.

4. Frustration

Frustration is like negative energy that eats up the good energy, sets you off track, and makes you lose inspiration. In short, negative energy should be avoided as much as possible.

I'm no expert but I can show you what I have done with it.

I have, for years now, always found the good in every bad situation. Now that can actually be frustrating for the people around you that don't think this way.

Here are examples of two small things that help me.

Hearing that song on the radio, in the store, at a party, or wherever you are that you like. You think that's a nice song and would love to have that. Yes, that starts a mental frustration in your mind, although maybe not as big as when you feel frustrated in a greater sense, but put together with other such small negative thoughts can eventually crash your entire day, and the outcome will be negative.

I use the app SoundHound that listens to the song, and almost always tells me what song it is. I then star-mark it on the app, and later someday when I have the time, I add it to an appropriate playlist on Spotify.

I use a mindmap where I have a photo that I took with my phone on all the lunch restaurants that I like. Having the photo makes it easier to decide when reading from a list. I grouped the restaurants based on the criteria of location. By doing this I have taken away some of the frustration of not knowing where to have lunch 5 days of the week.

Yes, I have done the same with dinner restaurants but have separated them in another mind-map.

Many people get really frustrated as they drive their cars. We can all probably understand that, as there are many different types of drivers in the traffic. You know it but many of us don't act the way we should as we do get frustrated, starting to scream in the car, knowing that the other driver cannot hear you anyway. So why do it? Just stop it as it only gets you fired up, increases your pulse, and has a negative impact on you. Think it through and you will realize that it's just not worth it. You might as well save that energy rush for something better like when you get home to your kids a few minutes later. Do you want to be angry or do you want to come home with positive energy?

Big or small, anytime I have a simple task that I have to do later, I write it up on a GPS based to-do list I use called 'App 2do'. I may include the small stuff like a reminder to buy milk or larger stuff such as my packing list for when I'm traveling. I may even include books I want to read in the future or movies I want to watch. Whenever I'm out and see something I'd like to have, I take a

By doing these simple things, I let go of the frustration in many areas and I can occupy my mind with other things.

In short, I design how I want to operate by taking care of the many distractions that we have throughout our days.

Inspiration

Inspiration is like food and energy for your brain. When inspired, you feel the energy, find new ideas popping up and solutions to issues that you have been struggling with earlier.

Identify what inspires you and turn to that when you are feeling down.

I get inspired and empowered by other people sharing their knowledge and experience when I listen to audiobooks and presentations on sites like Ted.com

Who inspires you?

Find people that inspire you and identify why they are inspiring to you.

I am inspired by many people and the one thing they all have in common is that they have done things that they have been taught and told is impossible.

Some people that I find inspiring are:

- Martin Luther King

  The famous "I have a dream" speech and how the world has evolved after that point.

- Ingvar Kamprad

  To start the first IKEA, he went to the municipal services in the area where he was living and asked for a plot of land for free, and in return he would give the residents in the area work opportunities, taking away some of the unemployment in the area.

- Daniel Tammet

  From his point of view, numbers are a language based on color and size, that float and interact with each other and are woven together as a new way of perceiving and understanding the world.

I have also learned that many successful people have dyslexia, and I looked into some of them and their way of thinking, and I can see similarities in terms of the will to prove people wrong and that we can do far more amazing things than most people "think" (I put that in quotes as I don't think people think they can't do these things, but they are taught to think that way).

Some of them are:

- Richard Branson
- Ingvar Kamprad
- Henry Ford
- Walt Disney
- Thomas Edison
- Alexander Graham Bell
- The list goes on...

You see it does not have to be one type of person that has the same goals but people whose lifestyle or ways of thinking speaks to you.

To fail is not to fail...

Failure doesn't necessarily mean that you were entirely wrong.

I have learned a lot from my failures. I learned that knowledge is never unnecessary but much of the knowledge is not essential.

What I mean is that we must feed our brains with knowledge, high and low, about everything. This knowledge or these experiences that in fact, is knowledge, we then use over and over again.

You do not need to store everything in your active brain necessarily. Put them in a corner spot in your brain but also understand how to use them when it's the time, because you might just come up with some extraordinary ideas thanks to those obscure pieces of information.

One of the hardest things for me is to learn to let go.

Many thoughts pass through our minds when we are thinking about letting go but one is obvious. "All the time I put into this, does this mean it's now just wasted time?"

Absolutely not. All the time you put into whatever it is that you did is a massive amount of experience and knowledge that you now will use and reuse in the most unlikely places, making what you thought earlier were impossible, possible. So, do dare to fail, as that's how we learned to walk as children, by failing but not giving up. Learn from those baby steps and improve step by step.

Stick your head out and work your ass off on an idea that you believe in. But to be able to work that much for an idea you have to first discover an idea you're passionate about.

Only then will you have a very different kind of work energy. You will know what I'm talking about once you find that idea and start believing in it with your soul.

I learned tenfold more when working with different business ideas than when I just did my basic daily work.

Don't be afraid to fail. As you now know how much you actually get out of daring to fail, you will welcome failure, as you understand it's just a learning curve for you to reach success.

If you're not afraid to fail, you will succeed with greater things. If you worry about failing and focus too much on the fallback plan or the safety net around your business plan, the probability is high that you will fail, as you haven't given enough time to the work needed to succeed.

The fisherman

I was told this story by Joakim, about whom I told you earlier in the book, and the story left a very lasting impression on me.

> *"When I visited Greece, I was walking around in the harbor where the ships are docked at night. There was only one boat there at that time, however, and I noticed that the fisherman was lying there with his boat, relaxed.*
>
> *So, asked him, 'Why are you not out fishing like all the other fishermen?'*
>
> *And he replied, 'Because I already caught the fish I need for the day.'*

I was baffled by the answer and replied to him, 'But you still have a long day ahead. If you keep fishing more, you might be able to earn more money. You could even afford to buy a bigger boat or a second boat and increase your earnings many-fold.'

To that, he replied, 'And what would I need that money for?'

I instantly replied, 'So that you could relax and enjoy the sun,' and just then I realized my stupidity."

My reflection from this story is to know your goal, yourself, and what you want in life. As what you want does not have to be what others around you want for you.

Your personality

We tend to believe that we know ourselves pretty well, but once-in-a-while, it's good to do some exercises to pick out the essence inside us and find what we want to focus on.

Here follows a list to get you started. Mark the ones you feel describes you.

I am good at/at being:

1. People person.
2. Systematic person.
3. Communication skills.
4. Leader.
5. Social person.
6. Problem solver.
7. Boosting other people.
8. Finding other people's strengths.
9. Understanding people's weaknesses.
10. Networking.
11. Giving feedback.
12. Team player.

13. Seeing obstacles before others.
14. Being a good father.
15. Being a good husband.
16. Teaching.
17. Memorizing things.
18. Encouraging people.
19. Learning.
20. Listening.
21. Learning from my mistakes.
22. Steadily improving myself.
23. Verbalizing my feelings.
24. Bringing out good things in others.
25. Doing more than is required.
26. Verbal expression.
27. Written language.
28. Learning a new language.
29. Forgiving.
30. Smiling.
31. Thinking positive.
32. Parenting.
33. Being a friend.
34. Punctual.
35. Doing what I say I will do.
36. Easy to speak with new people.
37. Giving good advice to people.
38. Know what I truly want.
39. Good at prioritizing.
40. Honest.

Add more to the list as you definitely have more to give with your amazing personality, than this shortlist. After reading through it your mind should get tuned into the type of thinking needed to identify your positive skills.

Summarize the marked ones by writing them down by hand on a list, and now you see your strengths and the things you should be proud of.

The importance of actually writing this down by hand lies in the hand movements involved that leave a motor memory in the sensorimotor part of the brain, which helps us recognize letters. This implies that there is a connection between reading and writing, and the sensorimotor system plays a role in the process of visual recognition when we read,

When I meet new people, I automatically think of how I can help them by sharing a particular experience or knowledge. This has been of great interest to me for many years now but I do realize that this is not always a good practice. Many times, people won't reciprocate as much as I'd like, in terms of sharing their experiences and knowledge with me.

But this is something that I'm working on changing, so for me to be able to learn and evolve, I came up with this newer fine-tuned model. In the future, as I meet with people that are interested in my experience and to receive guidance or help, I will ask them head-on about what they believe are their strengths and visions, and how I can learn from them.

Bucket list

As I realized that life is not all about work, I started to think about what I want with my life, and one of the easiest things to start with is to write a bucket list. It is usually much easier than writing a life plan, as the bucket list can consist of realistic and slightly crazier but attainable goals.

By writing a bucket list you get to know about yourself and what things you would like to do in life.

This is a great base for you to look back at, and once written down you will be surprised how many of the things you eventually get done. Writing down things in a list gets the list into your subconscious, and things do get done in another manner. Even more so, if you place that list somewhere where you see it every day. For example, you can put it on the inside of your wardrobe or even frame it and put it next to your coat rack or your mirror? So, don't just make up a list in your mind, take a pen and paper and write it down.

[GLUE:]

Treating yourself to the little successes is very important. Take a habit of yours that you like, but might want to minimize, and then do it only as a treat when you are satisfied with good work results. For example, you might like to consume Coca-Cola on regularly, but that is unhealthy and you know it. So, only when you have done excessively boring and tedious work, go out there and reward yourself with a bottle.

This will keep your health in better check without completely ruining your desires and also motivate you to do the menial tasks that you'd otherwise have no motivation to do at all. You will also feel much better about yourself knowing that you hit two birds with one stone and this will create positive energy inside you that will keep you going.

You just hacked your reward system.

Seventh section:
My experiences

The companies I started

Time expansion kit

My swimming experiences

Why hacking your Destiny

The journey of this book

Mastering a skill

First vs. Last Impression

Tools I use

Quotes

The companies I started

Let me tell you about the first two companies I started and the stories behind them. The goal is to motivate you and show you that even if it takes a lot of effort, it's not undoable.

Pixico

Pixico was the first company I started.

As I was only 16 at the time, starting a company as a minor was not an easy thing to do. First of all, starting a company at that age back in 1996 was almost unheard of, and I remember there was just one more guy of my age in the whole of Sweden that was trying to register his company. It started with friends to the family that was asking me for help with their computers and paid me in return. But instead of just giving me money, they felt it would be better if they could pay through an invoice sent by my company (which I did not have at that time) to their company. So, I started the process of registering a company at PRV (The Swedish Patents and Registrations Authorities).

In Sweden, you had to be 18 years old to register for a company at that time. So, there was a lot of struggle to get the paperwork done but with the help from my mother, we got it done. She wrote a bunch of letters to the PRV and acted as my guardian until I turned 18.

I worked at the time with every type of computer-related assignment as a consultant for private and smaller companies until I graduated from school.

I then got a full-time consultant assignment at Tele2. Following that, I got another offer from a newly started outsourcing company called X-source. I heard that they were planning to let go of all of their consultants.

I accepted their offer of becoming an employee, right after the meeting, I was approached by one of the older consultants who asked me if I accepted the offer. He then told me that this is the normal way of the business and all companies do this from time to time to minimize the costs and get some consultants as full-time employees instead. I felt like I got tricked but did not feel that bad about it as I did enjoy the company and what we accomplished as a team.

I came to look up to Joachim as some kind of experienced guidance, as he was satisfied with his position in life and I think that is one thing to strive for.

The name Pixico is actually from a game that our teacher introduced to us when we were in the 4th-6th grade. Pixico was the name of our made-up country and we, the students, were its citizens. Every day in school, we used to receive a salary in the form of 'Pix' which we could use to buy materials such as pens, sharpeners, papers, etc.

It was a great game that taught us much about real life. We had a king and a government and all that and realized how to take advantage of some parts in the system as some stole pens or money and some sold pens they got from home that was not part of the "economy". One time I and a friend bought the entire class "store" where the items like pens and papers were sold and then raised the price sky-high as we became the only store and held the monopoly.

This was a great practice that I think should be done in all schools to make children understand why their parents work and why the country works the way it does. Instead of plainly teaching it out, we understood it in real life, and we, instead of just accepting what we learned, also questioned it fundamentally.

So as this was the first connection I had to "grown-up life" this did fit perfectly for my new company and so the name Pixico was registered with PRV.

PID

PID Personal Interior Design was the second company that I started, and this time together with my closest friend Martin Wolf, but we did not get much further after the start.

Interior Design was a new domain for me and I had no experience at all but still, I tried to get into the field as I found it interesting, and wanted to learn about things that I did not know much about.

After abandoning the idea for a long time, I later restarted PID with my wife as we were both very interested in design.

It was a struggle as we did this in 2003 and the e-commerce field was largely affected by the IT boom and the design business was very much handled the old fashion way by people that had been in the business for larger parts of their life.

So, when we approached them, there was no positive feedback right from the get-go. We then sat down with them and explained how our business model worked and how they would benefit from being one of our suppliers.

It did take a tremendous amount of time and one great thing I did was that instead of going straight on the ones I wanted as suppliers, I wrote a list of several suppliers that were of interest and then started backward on the ones that were of low or no importance to us.

From each meeting, I learned a lot and got loads of experience and confidence.

So, when we approached the one we were looking forward to working with, we both had a list of suppliers that we already started working with. So, we were no small startup, and I had fine-tuned the "pitch" so it was as good as it could get. I had answers to any question that they could think of, as I had already heard them so many times before by then.

At first, we used a low-priced e-commerce application that built static HTML pages that were uploaded to the webserver.

I soon realized that the first e-commerce platform did not work as expected, so I started writing on a mind map with the PID 2.0 e-commerce platform demands.

It resulted in a list of about 200 pages with specific requirements and details about every element on the site.

We then split the project up so that the "engine" could be developed and put to work ASAP. This was done by Stefan Westling, a great Swedish Developer.

It did cost a lot of money for us but it was well worth it.

When we had the engine up and running, we started outsourcing work to India to do the rest of what was specified in the PID 2.0 mind map.

The project was given to an Indian development company and to start with the work went well, and we had a large number of developers working on the project.

I soon realized that they were not holding the project together well and that their employees were changing frequently inside the company. After some research, I learned that they counted work experience in months and not years as we do, and employees leaving for other opportunities without much notice was a common occurrence.

This became a problem as we had to teach the new developers about our setup over and over again.

So, I approached the developers that produced the best result in the project and offered them the project on the side.

I employed them max-time which meant as many hours as they could, which normally was about 6-8 hours per day 6-7 days a week.

They did not quit their day-job, but worked with me after their normal office hours.

One great thing to know about outsourcing to India is that they listen to the customers' demands and understand their requirements very well.

A few things to think of as you outsource to low-cost countries and its benefits:

1. Read about the country and understand its structure.
2. Read about their culture and try to understand the difficulties and issues that might lie ahead.
3. Search on LinkedIn to see if you could have a chat with someone that has experience in outsourcing something similar to the country that you want to outsource to.

The price could be 1/10 or even less of the work being done in your country.

Doing what you are told is good but doing so without questioning at all, turns out to be counter-productive in the long run, so I had to find a way to deal with that.

I would explain only a part of what I wanted, and then they had to fill in the gaps, and explain back to me what I actually wanted. It then got them to think on their own and with their programming experience.

To get them up to speed with this method it took about 6 months, but it was well worth it as we then worked perfectly together as a team.

We looked after products worldwide and after a while designers started reaching out to us asking to have their products on the PID website.

We did a lot of work with the press contacts and it really paid off, instead of paying for ads we had products in almost every interior design magazine in Sweden every month and many magazines worldwide where we were mentioned on the cover with product images as the first-page cover.

We worked hard on all fronts to get known and it did work well, but we did work very hard to get to that point.

The expansion was always our main focus.

We had the entire site translated to 12 languages and shipped products worldwide.

Google was by no means an easy task but after a hard struggle and many long nights, we did get on the first search result for many of our keywords.

SEO is a tricky business. You have to do it right from the start for you to expect it to work.

If you do it wrong, you will get banned or black-listed. Remember your entire business relies on customers searching for the products you have.

At one point we decided to open a physical store. This was a risky task but again one we learned loads from doing it.

But as our customer base was mostly international, a physical store would only attract customers in the local area.

After about one year we decided to close that physical store down and focus on the web-store.

We did put in more time than money came out from PID, as the market still was not ready to shop interior design online in the wide spectra that we needed.

We did have 2000 visitors per day but had no large orders. Customers were only buying smaller things for normally less than 3000 Swedish kronor.

One thing I did when I started building PID is that I looked at everyone, our competitors (there were only two at that time), and many other e-commerce sites globally to see what they did and what they did not do.

I struggled hard to design a site that did work as the customers would naturally expect it and not as every other e-commerce site. It took a long time as I wanted to find the natural way, not the standard way. Everything had to be intuitive and hidden so that the user had to look after it, whatever function it was.

So do learn from your competitors' good and bad things. Try to observe what they do or don't and then understand the reason behind that. You might even want to contact them and ask them directly.

Be sure to build your own thing.

I tend to get back to this. If you copy someone, you should be sure to know why you are doing it and what primary goals are, as by copying you won't get further than they have, and you surely will learn less than they have.

But to copy someone just because it's so easy and stupid to not do it as there might be room for competition within the same market then that's not guaranteed to be a dumb idea. You do not always have to be unique or authority and that's important to be aware of.

While trying to be unique, however, one must also remember that there will be others who would try to copy from your work.

We had this same problem as many websites copied our product descriptions straight off our site and Google doesn't take content duplication lightly. So, we had to make sure that our entire site was indexed by Google so that we would not get penalized for other people copying us.

Naming and Logo

The name is at least as important as the logo.

I took the following steps when picking the name for my company:

1. Write a list of inspiring words that could speak as a description of what the company does or wants to communicate.
2. Then look at the list and let your subconscious come up with names. Sometimes they may not even have to literally mean anything sounds good and appropriate.
3. Don't think too much about it, just brainstorm; write down whatever comes to your mind and then after a day or two, go back to the list and read it through. Remove the points that you don't feel for and group some of the ones you find best as a top 10 list.
4. Check the domain. Many of the names are probably already taken on the .com domain so then just remove them or find a suitable variant that is available. See if the variant still stands strong compared to the rest of the list.

5. Now do a pool. See what people around you think about the name without saying what the company will do at first. Use any of the large numbers of poll-sites available out there and publish your poll on Facebook or LinkedIn to see peoples' votes and comments.

Now to the logo. For the logo, I did actually just the same.

I did the brainstorm of inspiration and reused the naming list too.

I also Googled around to see other logos, I checked my competitors and looked into their logos if were widely used in the area the company would deliver in.

When I had a description and samples of logos that I did like, I published it all on 99designs.com to have some experts do what they do best, design a bunch of different logos for me, and then pick the best one after doing some smaller modifications.

Time Expansion Kit

Q: How can I maximize the time I have for productive work, and better handle my companies?

Trying to find an answer to this question, I came up with a strategy that I will share with you.

Not every single idea that comes to your mind motivates you to work endlessly towards achieving it but every once-in-a-while there'll be one such idea that you would treat like a baby and care for. And when you don't perform well towards achieving it, you feel really sad and frustrated.

For the majority of my working life, I had been working at two jobs because of which I had very little time to focus on my personal goals. I realized I had to expand the time that I could put into my company and my clients, so I created what I called my time expansion kit.

It's basically a combination of methods that I came up with to trick my body to not go into rest.

I did this by starting in my home while eating breakfast. I realized that I could change my breakfast time to a little later.

I then waited with my lunch until 14:00 and used the meantime to do some work. When I came home, I did not stop but kept working directly without slowing down and by doing so, I never let my body get into the relax mode.

Now obviously, this is something that I can't recommend everyone to do, as it puts your body under intense pressure.

I had my supper at about 22:00 or 23:00 and went to bed at 01:00 at night.

There were two basics to this:

1. Don't eat when you normally do. The idea behind this is to not let your body know what stage of the day it is. Thus, you confuse yourself out of times when you would naturally want to rest.
2. Throw out TVs and other such distractions. This will increase the general available time you have for yourself to work towards your goals.

Don't slow down. Normally everyone slows down when they get home from work and this affects the entire delivery. I had no strict milestones for the company PID and I always just wanted to make it more successful. This did cause large problems in the long run, however.

What I should have done was to have different project goals which I then combined into different milestones.

Example:

- Sales per day should be minimum X orders
- The sales should increase by X% every month
- We should have x products in the year X
- We should have x registered users in the year X

It would then have been easier to find what was needed to be done to the site and the business model to reach those goals.

But in reality, I would have needed a business plan with the milestones integrated. I would have to sit down and create a plan which would take time and hard work. But in the end, it would be worth it as it works as the thin red line that you must follow to reach the goal.

I have learned to stick to doing what I do best. Of course, that does not mean you cannot learn new skills, or that you should not venture out into other fields. But as we have limited time and resources, to meet personal goals in defined deadlines, we need to understand how to balance acquiring new skills and making do with what we already have. In the end, you have to focus on the key things and if you stray too far, it may become a difficult road to achieving your goals.

Try to understand what you expect out of the business and how much you are willing to work on achieving that goal.

You now have set some basic rules for how and what to do with the company which will be of great use to you as it evolves.

I did not want to just start a consultant company. I wanted to do it right, have the answers to my future employees before they got hired. So, I spent a lot of time building up the company base structure instead of just building some card house. I have seen many companies that are just like empty card houses; they look good on the outside, but as an employee, you soon realize that that's just the selling buzzwords that sounded good in the beginning.

But before that, I suggest you do an exercise where you create a bullet list (or a mind map) of all the things you need, and then estimate the time each part might take and any problems you might think of that you will face.

I built a great base and frame for the company but realized that the complexity was for me to find people that answered up to my high set goals of experience, professionalism, and personality. Simply put I was looking for people like me to hire. But the problem was that people like me were not looking for employment, they were already running their own companies.

My swimming experiences

We have visited and revisited this topic so many times through-out the journey of this book, but we shall do it one last time. I want you to really understand the risks and the fact that even though it sounds simple enough, it can be a very overwhelming experience.

Swimming. Yes, nothing fancy but let me tell you this is prob-ably the second-best thing I have done to educate myself. And you will be able to read the long or the short story here. If you like to hear the long story just keep reading. If you want to focus on the things that give you value for the time spent you can skip over the next chapter and the topic "The result."

It all started on a sunny summer day. Two of my colleagues and I were out walking after lunch, and instead of walking back, we decided to swim back. There was a jetty packed with people and we only had one plastic bag which we used to pack all of our stuff to prevent them from getting soaked. Dag started swimming and after about 20 meters, Rolle and I realized that Dag was sinking, like something was slowly pulling him down.

We could not stop laughing. Now when you start laughing as you swim, you may have difficulty in maintaining the proper strokes or trying to keep yourself afloat.

Rolle was closest to Dag, so he picked up the bag that just touched the surface and Dag was not visible as he was under the surface trying to hold the bag away from the surface.

Rolle swam 10 meters, and then the same thing happened to him. Next, I grabbed the bag and swam 10 meters, and the same happened to me as well. So about 40 meters from the jetty, we realized that we would drown if we tried to swim to all of 500 meters trying to keep the bag from soaking.

So, we decided to turn back to the jetty and all the people there were just baffled with what we just did and did not understand why we sank and what just happened. It must have looked so crazy from their point of view.

Now I'm not really a quitter, so I did some thinking about what I did wrong and what I can do better to achieve the goal, and swim the 500 meters with this plastic bag full of clothes the next day. We went back with new knowledge about how rescue-swimmers swim while supporting another person in the water.

We jumped in the water and started swimming on our back and with the weight on our breast, and we were successful. We got the entire 500 meters without any problem at all.

We then got stubborn and focused on swimming like we did at first, but switched carriers after just a few meters, and we eventually reached the original goal and swam the entire 500 meters with the bag above water using just chest swim.

As this was a great workout and fun too, I invited Dag and Rolle to this in their calendar and set the last repetitive date to be the first of November

It was the first of November 2010 and the last day of our swimming lunches.

We realized that we did not have that big of a problem with the cold water, so instead of being content with achieving a second goal, we went ahead and set up the third one.

Rolle had left us as the water turned colder, but Dag and I were still going strong. We had changed our route slightly for security reasons. We checked the water temperature and it was now 8 Celsius and the swimming of the now 600 meters took about 20 minutes including one pit stop.

We swam 300 meters and then got up on a jetty to do 30 elevated push-ups to increase the blood circulation in our body. Following that, without any rest, we jumped into the water and swam the 300 meters back.

Since we only had our swim trunks on, we did get rather cold. It normally stings when you swim for about the first 50 meters but slowly the body starts to adapt to the new temperature. After that, you only feel cold when you actually step out of the water.

We then jogged 400 meters to the showers and at the same time as we showered, we drank a cup of green tea.

Even though the tea was nearly cold, our bodies were so chilled that it really felt warm to us and the shower helped us bring our body temperature back to normal.

During the unfreezing process, you might feel a bit sick, but this is just something mental. You might also feel dizzy, and I learned that in situations like these, one should not sit down as that might cause them to pass out leading to injuries.

Winter swimming

During the swimming, we kept a close watch on each other and small talked all the time to see that the partner was on track, and not feeling dizzy or having problems with speech somehow.

We also checked before every swim that both were 100% okay with it and that we did not feel ill or had physical limitations one way or another. We were concerned and made sure that we put no pressure on each other which might make us push ourselves to risky areas we might not be able to handle in this extreme situation.

We never experienced this, but were well aware that if the synchronized swimming movement was not working in perfect coordination, it was a sign that our bodies were shutting down and it would be best to get out of the water.

If you start doing jumps or squats immediately after a swim, you risk having what is called Past Rescue Collapse. You would lose consciousness and fall backward onto the ground, which is believed to happen due to the blood becoming cold and thick, making it hard to reach up to the brain.

What you do out of happiness normally acts as life support in extreme situations like this.

Sometimes, getting out of the water would seem tough in itself because of how cold the air would feel. Other times, when we climbed up the metal ladders, the frozen metal would make our skin stick to the metal, and freeing the hand from such a situation proved to be quite a difficult task. This happens because the water on our body is about 2-3 Celsius in that situation, whereas the air around us is easily around -17 Celsius or lower, so when our skin came into contact with the metal it would freeze instantly.

After a while, we changed the length from 1000 meters to 600 meters, and eventually down to 300 meters where we would swim laps instead.

While going into the water, we always dove with our hands first. When we tried to jump into the water, but after even a meter or two, it would get very cold. So, we did some tests to see what could be done to fix this.

We jumped into the water with our feet first, and as you do that you flap your arms as you reach the surface with no synchronized movement that is connected to your breathing.

This gave the defect of the loss of our controlled breathing, and we actually started hyperventilating for the first time. After a few seconds of focus, we did control the breathing again but realized that jumping in the water feet-first is even worse than jumping with your head first.

One other thing when diving in is that the water hits your central nervous system first and at the speed of electricity your entire body is set to handle the situation at hand. When jumping with your feet first, it takes far longer to get your body to set for the challenge.

Even after we shortened the distance, we did get cold and our skin ended up feeling like chain-armor because of it. After a while, our body loosened up slightly again, and it got easier to swim for a few minutes.

Then something happened that we were always told should not happen. We have all heard about 'survival instinct'; it's a phenomenon where our subconscious mind takes control of our body to keep us alive. Right after we jumped into the water, our subconscious mind almost took over because of this instinct, wanting to find a way out of there. But since we were prepared for it, we fought it and kept our consciousness and instead, started swimming. Had I stopped swimming at that point, I'd have most probably sunk peacefully to the bottom.

At that point, it was obvious to us how important our determination to chase the goal was to keep us alive. We kept swimming until we reached that goal, which was the edge of the open water, where the ice took over the frozen lake.

As I had already mentioned, our toes and fingers were frozen. As we made back for the office, our toes felt like cracking against the asphalt below.

We solved this problem the next time, however, using neoprene gloves and socks.

When swimming, we realized that it was really important to not let the brain freeze too much. You can get the back of your head swollen and it hurts a lot non-stop. Also, the wet hair from diving into the water was a problem. We fixed it by wearing a rubber swimming cap. The water did not circulate in direct contact with our heads, which helped us to maintain the temperature. We were still wearing swimming trunks though, but we added a layer to minimize the contact with water.

As the water temperature went down, we could feel the change of even 0.5 Celsius and could analyze and understand more in detail how it affected us.

One very interesting result was the feeling we got about 30 minutes after the swim. As we swam, our brain seemed to drop all other thoughts and focused on only one thing: staying alive.

Our brain flushed all active thoughts and focused on surviving, because of which our memories were really hazy. Our minds were blank when we got out of the water eventually, and we could later tell that our brain was working at full capacity to try to focus on that single task, because of which it abandoned any other thoughts.

After we got out of the water, we did some leveled push-ups before we jogged back to the office and took a shower. We then got ready and when we stepped out of the changing room, we felt like we had survived the challenge and our entire body relaxed.

When you jump into cold water or take a cold shower, your body intensely flexes every single muscle in your body. Your whole body gets a workout, not from lifting weights, but simply from flexing the muscles. After a while, the body adapts and relaxes the muscles. As a result, your whole body feels relaxed completely.

Another thing our body experiences after such an exercise is that the energy reserves we maintain are drained, and this is interesting as we become mentally aware of how much energy we have left as it nears depletion levels. But even though we may feel that it is just our brain tricking us into believing that we have run out of energy, where in reality that's not the case. We might go through this several times before we actually run out of energy.

This is the thing that happens when you go to the gym. You lift the weight, for example, 18 kg dumbbells, and you do 15 reps. Now your mind tells you 15 is enough and that you can't produce more than 15 reps. You can almost always tell yourself that you can do 2 more if you have someone standing by your side. If that person doesn't back down but helps you by just touching your elbow you can probably do even 3 more. The person helping you is not really lifting even a kilo, but your brain believes you are getting help and therefore, can produce more energy.

So where does that energy come from?

Upon some thought, it is clear that the energy we can produce is split up in different containers and can be used in different situations.

It's easiest to explain it like this: if personal safety level 1 is breached, then use depot 2 to stabilize the situation. Depot 2 can't be used if personal safety level 1 is not actually breached and therefore, you have no control or even mental knowledge about its existence until you have used up every single bit of energy in the depot that is safety level 1.

When we swim, we breach almost every one of these "personal security levels" and can thus make use of all the energy our body can produce or has reserved for critical situations.

When we are done, we experience a unique kind of feeling that is best described as if you were sleeping for a week, and then wake up totally relaxed. Your body feels like new and you feel unusually relaxed.

Burning fat

In the cold water, our bodies were forced to produce heat constantly to keep the body temperatures as high as possible. To produce heat, our body burns fat to produce more energy.

We never realized how effective this exercise would be in disposing of unnecessary fats, but looking at the results, we were really shocked when we checked ourselves in front of a mirror.

Now, neither Dag nor I am the kind of person that has too much unnecessary fat in our bodies, so when our bodies ran out of fat to burn as a result of trying to keep us alive, it started to burn muscles as well.

This was not really something we wanted. So, after realizing this, we tried to fill up our bodies with fast protein every day before the swim so that our body would use that instead which helped to stabilize the situation.

What we learned about cold water swimming

In October, we contacted the Swedish sea rescue society and talked to a person named Anders and described to him what we were doing. He told us what he knew but also that he did not know much about what happens in water under 10°C.

We have kept swimming to the freezing point in the water and the water does get to around 2°C just before it turns to flaky ice and then to solid ice.

If a person falls into the water involuntarily, their body can immediately go into a shock, and they might start to hyperventilate, which would soon lead to the person passing out in the water which then leads to the drowning.

It's totally different, however, if you intentionally jump into the water, as you will have enough time to prepare mentally beforehand and most probably won't go into shock. That said, your heart will be working much harder and blood will become much more sluggish than normal. It is thus really important that you don't have any kind of medical history revolving around the heart if you wish to try this.

If you feel vigorous shivering, be careful that your body might be running out of fuel to produce heat, and it might be dangerous to stay in the water any longer. If you quickly rise up from a sitting position, you will most probably pass out. When you regain consciousness, you'll probably feel like you are drunk and your balance system is out of order.

Conclusion

If you are about to rescue someone in the water, swim on your back with the victim on your chest.

If you're in a situation where a boat might go under or you risk falling into the water, it is much better to take the mental decision to jump in the water as it will increase your survival chances greatly.

Dive into the water and do not jump with your feet first.

Use neoprene gloves and socks.

Don't do it alone, do it with someone you trust.

What I learned from my swimming experiences is that everything is possible. Have goals. Having multiple goals is even better, but also learn to focus on the closest goal first, so that you can stay on track and achieve those goals efficiently.

Why hacking your Destiny

This book opened with the concept of hacking your destiny, so let me elaborate on it in case you haven't already found the answers naturally through this book.

But before we jump into the concept of destiny, I'd like to talk about what makes us who we are. This is perhaps a more spiritual or philosophical question that most of us have probably thought about at some point in life or in other. When I talk about "me" or any other person, we see that as one entity; a person is who he or she is, right?

I have been pushing myself in many different ways during my life in attempts to learn more about myself or perhaps redis-cover who I am, or who we are for that matter.

According to me, the "me" consists of 5 elements. I will try to explain below with a few examples of what they are and how they interact with each other in different situations.

1. My free will.
2. My intellectual brainpower and previous experiences.
3. My subconscious mind.
4. The Brain.
5. The Body.
6. Stay alive, protection system
7. The spirit of me, the soul
8. The energy of me, the gut feeling, the 6th sense.

Example 1: If I decide to stop eating sugar, I will still have an urge for sugar for some time. This is my brain trying to take control over my free will and tell me to get sugar into my sys-tem again, as the brain lives on fast carbs and is the laziest and most energy-consuming organ in the body.

It might even try to move my body when I'm in other thoughts, trying to control the movement to make it easier to get some sugar.

I can then go in and take control of my brain and mentally lower the urge.

Example 2: In the gym when I am working out, I might define how many repetitions I want to do of that particular exercise.

It's easy to pick 10, but to push myself, I may pick 12 and then I try to persuade my body to keep up. But I don't count from 1-12 as that hints my brain that I'm trying to break my barrier.

So instead, I divide it into smaller parts to make it feel easier. For example, 4X3 repetitions without a pause, during the exercise my body will speak with my brain telling it that it's ok to stop. After a short while, the brain will then agree as it always thinks it's good to conserve energy for any cases of emergency or danger. This was something developed in our bodies from when we were cavemen and "real" life-threatening dangers were more common than they are these days.

At that point, it's up to my free will, which already reasoned with my intellectual mind under my control and where I came to the conclusion and defined the goal of 12 repetitions.

I then tell my mind to stop complaining and my mind then tells my body to keep going, sort of like giving up their attempt to change your mind.

Example 3: Let's assume you have a bar of chocolate. You say to yourself that you will have just one bite and save it for later. Here, you used your free will to make a decision.

But as soon as you take that one bite, your brain tries to take control. It will make you want to have one more bite. And then one more.

Again, this is because the brain is lazy and always wants fast carbohydrates, and sugar is one of the easiest ones for the brain to use. That's why it tries to override your previously defined limitation.

Example 4: Let's say that you are in a traffic accident. One of the things that happen is that your mind, which is normally full of active thoughts and memories, is wiped clean to make use of your full brainpower. As you do this, it feels like time slows down but in reality, it's just that you are uncluttering your thoughts and all your senses are focused on one thing only, the current situation. You then block impressions that are irrelevant to the situation; basically, only collecting information about the closest things and your subconscious is scanning for things that might affect your current limited bubble of information. If it finds anything, the bubble will include that part too. For example, it might be a second car coming in from another site that might hit you too if you don't do something about it. But you don't notice the trees on the side, as your subconscious mind has already made a threat assessment and decided that the probability is low that those things could cause a threat in that microsecond.

We covered parts of it in the chapter about the speed of thoughts as you might remember.

During these situations, your brain makes rapid and focused calculations and controls your body's movement and everything else to make sure that its "host" stays alive. Without the "host" the stay alive system will die, which is its only defined goal to never accept.

Your body also has stored energy in energy reserves; these you will never be able to access with your intellectual mind. And the "stay alive" system will keep them hidden from your knowledge even. They are saved for when they are needed, and they have amazing powers.

Combined with that the body also has adrenaline that makes your body even stronger, faster, and alert but for a short while.

From my personal experiences, I can say that when "the stay alive energy" reserves are exhausted, there are, to my knowledge, two more layers of hidden energy reserves, which again are hidden and not known until you are in a situation where all the previous reserves have been exhausted.

There are so many more examples that I can give you, but instead, try to think on your own about what kind of situations you might face and how you want to deal with them. I am confident that you will find multiple situations every day, but it might take a little time to know how to see when it's happening.

To understand these layers is one of the keys to hacking your destiny; to understand why things are the way they are, and how come your life evolves the way it does.

By understanding these layers, you will find it as useful as when you first understood the difference between your feet and your hands. They are all used for different things and great at their thing, but they are not great at everything. They are strong when combined and that combination is YOU.

Take a moment and think about that! Be proud that no matter who you are, you are unique, amazing, and can do anything. So, use your free will to define a goal, incorporate your intellectual brainpower to make a plan, and work your body and your sub-conscious to start working towards that plan.

What you will see is that your brain again starts to interfere, as it seems that you are suddenly using up more energy on new activities; and as you remember, the brain is the laziest part of your body. It just wants to conserve energy for all the if and but situations.

[GLUE:]

Here are some ways for you to find this out on your own. You will see how the different elements I mentioned try to take control of you.

Go through the following list to get some inspiration and ideas about potential topics to work on. Try different diets to trigger your mind to act and react in different ways.

Ketogenic diet: Your mind will tell you to eat anything with carbohydrates, your body will tell you to sleep to conserve energy and you will be in closer contact with the different layers that we just discussed.

Fasting: If you skip a meal or two, your mind will tell you to do anything to get food. You will feel depressed and lose interest in things that previously interested you. You will be surprised how your survival instinct makes you more creative to make sure that you meet your body's requirements.

Stop a bad habit, smoking, sugar, alcohol, or any other addictive habits. Listen to your brain and your body. What is it saying? What is it trying to make you do? Do you agree with what it's saying or are you being pushed in a direction that you did not choose?

According to an experiment first conducted by Dr. MacDougall in 1907, in which he measured a few patients' bodies before and after they died, the average weight of a human soul is 21 grams. Now, some people may believe this to be true and others may not, but since this experiment was conducted well over 100 years ago, we can't say much about its authenticity or reliability.

I'm no expert in this field, but I believe that I do have a soul although I would not say that it's part of my physical body and

181

thus, it would most probably carry no weight. Yet, I believe it is there in some form.

The soul is not a definition of our destiny. Destiny is a word, remember this to start with. It's a word that has been invented just like the word impossible. It's invented to describe something and, in this case, according to the most trusted word-books of the world the meaning of the word is:

"The events that will necessarily happen to a particular person or thing in the future." -**Cambridge.**

"The force that some people think controls what happens in the future, and is outside human control."

"A person's destiny is everything that happens to them during their life, including what will happen in the future, especially when it is considered to be controlled by someone or something else."

"Destiny is the force which some people believe controls the things that happen to you in your life."

But as I investigated some more around this specific word, I found many contradicting explanations like:

destiny

/'dɛstɪni

Origin

Middle English: from Old French destinee, from Latin destinata, feminine past participle of destinare 'make firm, establish'.

My conclusion is that the word destiny, which originates from French, was invented to describe someone who was on a firm destination to establish a factual state for his or herself, which to me sounds like we are using the word "Destiny" in the wrong way these days.

Destiny is not a predefined state that we can't maneuver or can't affect or change. It describes a potential future, but a future that you could control or even lose control of. You can change during the journey of your life and define your own future.

I have covered many different topics in this book but to sum it all up I have written it to inspire you to take control of your destiny, define your own goals and be aware that you chose the path that leads to them.

"Travel beyond your horizons, and you will find there are no limits. Only endless possibilities."

-Karl Lillrud

The journey of this book

When I started writing this book, I had no vision of how long I actually wanted this book to be but since I wanted to write a proper book, I knew a few pages wouldn't suffice. By working dynamically with a mindmap I could let my inspiration flow freely, and in a later stage, choose which topics I like to combine and include in the book. By doing so, it also helped me open up my mind and make room for new ideas and other interesting things.

I would like to thank you for giving me so much of your highly valued time. I have intended to make sure that the time you have invested in reading this book has a positive outcome in many ways, and that you acquire the proper tools and knowledge that can help you in making decisions that will save you time and in the process, develop a better and much more efficient lifestyle.

Also, please feel free to send me feedback through any of my contact options. I love the feedback! Some might be harsh for sure but as long as its feedback, and not just criticism, it's something I can learn and evolve from. Even the teacher learns from their students every day.

After finishing the book, I suggest that you take some time to really reflect on the new things you may have learned by reading this book and try to figure out which points could help you improve your own life and how. Tweak my methods to fit into your life and start doing new things. Take up your phone and add a note in your calendar three months from now, so that after three months you can take a look back and reflect on what ways you have improved, and in what ways you can improve furthermore.

Put another note on the calendar, but one year from now that says you should review your time plan and celebrate your improvements and success. This will help keep yourself on-track during a larger time-span.

Last but not least. What's next? You now know a lot about me and my experiences. So, what would you like to know more about? If you require any advice, tips, ideas, reflections, glue tests, or anything you want to share, feel free to reach out to me without any hesitation.

Why I believe writing your own book would do you good:

As I wrote in the intro, this book is a project I pushed onto myself, just like I'm recommending you. By doing so, I have found many questions I wanted to ask myself and also found the answers to them. It has meant a great deal to me and I have learned a lot from it.

I encourage you to start by writing a short presentation about why you think and act the way you do, or how have come you value the things you value. You will then start viewing yourself, the people around you, and your overall life in a new light.

I hope that after you have finished reading this book you will have a new outlook on life, and maybe find new questions and answers within yourself which will make you think deeper about who you really are.

My goals

Mentor

As you know by now, I really enjoy helping people and sharing my experience and findings in ways that can help and support them. As a person with experience in many different fields, I can often discuss ideas and tips with almost anybody conversing on almost any topic.

As a consultant, my profile has evolved from being an expert to becoming a mentor, someone who guides people to success.

If you are interested in learning more about the mentorship program you should pick up your phone and go to www.karllillrud.com and schedule the first call with me right now. Don't postpone it; do it right now as this is the most important message I can give to you through this book: **time is money**.

Investor

I live for ideas, but personally, I can't perform all of them by myself. Hence, I like to be part of future ideas as an investor and advisor.

If you are looking for investors, you can read more about that on my website too.

I'm always keeping my mind active by running several ideas; some may call it ventures and some call them startups. With limited time, I am always looking for people that have the power and interest of doing some amazing and creative work together with me.

Mastering a skill

The 10,000 hours rule by Malcolm Gladwell states that it takes 10000 hours of work/training on a specific task before one is an expert at what he or she does. This is a number that was reached upon based on studies revolving various chess players, violinists, tennis players, etc.

For me, it took me 15 years in work-life to find what I wanted to do. It took me 15 years to believe in my own capacity and my ways of thinking.

Today, I'm 40 years old and my only real advice is to never stop asking why.

Don't give a fuck

Listen to everybody but don't learn from everybody. Even as some share their knowledge, it does not mean that their knowledge fits where you are in your life and in the things you do. But do listen, as you might find a use for it in the future one way or another.

[GLUE:] Mantra

Write your own mantras down on a paper and repeat them over and over again; put it up on the wall, so that your eyes pass by them every day, repeating it in your subconscious.

Design some nice-looking affirmation framings that you can put up on the wall or in a frame on your table.

Mine are:

- Nothing is impossible
- Never give up
- There are more roads than the one obvious or previously known
- Learn every day
- Find alternative solutions
- Make sure my family is not in the second room

First vs. Last Impression

The image you saw at the beginning of the book is of me, the author. After reading this far, I believe you probably know me a bit better than when you started this book. Thus, I want you to repeat the exercise from the beginning in which I asked you to write down key points that come to your mind from looking at the photo.

The key, again, is to write down what you think directly and not over-process your thoughts, just let your inner mind speak to you and write it down. I call it the First impression vs Last impression test. This helps in understanding what parts of someone's character stands out to us and how it affects the first impreison.

You can now compare the two lists you made and see how your thoughts about me have changed. You can apply this to your life as well, and see how people view you on first interaction to know more about what it is about you that stands out and how you might want to change it.

If you don't mind, I would love for you to share the two lists you made to me. You can just upload them on Instagram and tag my handle "@keynotekarl" to it, or find me on LinkedIn with my name, Karl Lillrud, and share it to me.

I am greatly interested in learning about your first impression, and see if that has changed from taking part in this journey in the search of answers together with me.

Tools I use:

Mindmeister: Web-based and app for mind mapping powerful and easy to use at the same time.

https://www.mindmeister.com/

Google apps: The obvious cloud-based office pack, there are also alternatives like Office 365 and Zoho.

https://gsuite.google.com/

Cloud storage: Google Drive is the obvious choice for you to use if you use their App suite. Consider looking into Dropbox as a separate alternative.

Degoo: 200GB of online cloud drive perfect as an extra backup solution.

https://degoo.com/keynotekarl

Grammarly: Spelling and grammar check using artificial intelligence and natural language processing.

https://app.grammarly.com/

LastPass: The password manager that generates and stores encrypted passwords for you to access from any device. https://www.lastpass.com/

2Do: iPhone app that has all the functionality you could dream of for to-do lists including GPS positioning which reminds you of what to do when you're at a specific location.

Audio book apps like Storytel, Amazon and Audible: Audiobooks streamed to your smartphone with the possibility to increase the playback speed.

Spreeder: Web App that speeds up your reading extremely.

https://www.spreeder.com/app.php

If this then that: Web App that I use to manage many automatic tasks and monitoring of whatever I feel like, for example, some specific word in my LinkedIn feed, give it a try or use many of the ready-made recipes.

http://ifttt.com/

Buffer: Web app that I use to publish my posts on the social media sites I use and with the ability to schedule when the posts are done.

https://buffer.com/

99designs.com: Design tasks that for a low cost, connect you with a massive amount of graphic designers that can do your logo, business cards, or whatever else you need to have done in graphics.

The nifty thing with 99designs is that your task is run as a competition where several freelancers compete for your prize money and where only one is named the winner of the prize money that you set when publishing the project.

In terms of outsourcing, I also use Guru, Freelancer, Fiverr, and People per hour. The choice of platform depends on what I want to do, what budget I have, and how much time I have to spend.

I publish many small tasks to do test runs, to collect data or customer expectations and requirements before I start a new venture. And with the resources that these platforms provide, I can analyze my business idea in a better way before I start investing much money into it.

Mindfulness, Sleep analytics, and breathing apps

I would like to say that this is something that you should find out on your own as it's rather personal. Download a couple of apps and play around with them and set up a goal, let's say that you use one app 3 times per day to see if you like how it looks and feels.

The ones I have used are:

To analyze my sleeping patterns I use https://www.sleepcycle.com/

To train your breathing and learn how to meditate I suggest you download the app Headspace https://www.headspace.com/

I will cover many more tools and how to make use of them in detail in the next book that I'm working on so make sure you go to https://www.karllillrud.com/ and subscribe to the future book releases.

Quotes

Quotes are something that I think you should have a second glance at. They work as affirmations and inspiration. They help you keep focused and believe in what you are doing.

Find the ones that you feel empowered by and get back to them every now and then, it could be that you have them in a frame at your desk or on the inside of your wardrobe or somewhere else where you see them every now and then.

Below are some quotes that have truly inspired me during tough times and helped me improve myself as a person. I hope you can accept them into your life and learn from them as well.

- **It is often said that "Behind Every Great Man Stands a Strong Woman"**

  I recently heard another one that was new to me but also very true "Behind every successful man is a surprised woman."

- **"Everything can be copied except your passion."**

  Think about this for a minute. Instead of just reading and agreeing you soon realize that this is a great truth and something to live by. If you have a passion you can do whatever you believe in but if you lack passion then you can easily be outrun by your competitors.

- **"Do it with passion or not at all**
  -Rosa Nochette Carey

  It's so true, always do the things you are passionate about as that's where you will get the best results and most out of your life.

- **"They did not know it was impossible, so they did it"**
  -Mark Twain

  I just love this one by Mark Twain, it's the essence of what I'm talking about so much, don't tell everyone about limitations, and they will not follow them or be held back by them.

We have almost reached the end of this book, but still we are far from the end.

I have written several books and I believe that if you have read this far the other books might interest you too.

Go to www.KarlLillrud.com to find them all and subscribe to be notified of future releases.

Are you interested in getting the next book for free?

Then just take a selfie with you and the book, audio book or ebook and send to me with a short note telling me what you liked about it as a testimonial that I have your permission to use in my marketing.

To show my gratitude I will give you my next book for free!

I am personally so grateful and happy that you have read my book. I always want you to give more, and even as we are on the last page I have even more to give to you.

By visiting https://www.karllillrud.com/hacking-your-destiny/extras you find the digital extras that I have prepared to get more out of the glue exercises only for you who have read my book.

Go and check it out to get even more out of the investment you have made in yourself by reading Hacking your destiny.

I also invite you to join my online mentor program here and every now and then i give out free sessions. Just go to the mentor tab on www.KarlLillrud.com and book your first session.

Follow me in social media:
https://www.linkedin.com/in/karllillrud/
https://www.instagram.com/keynotekarl/
https://twitter.com/karllillrud

Help me help you!

One of the most important things to learn is to listen, so now as you have "listened" to me by reading my words I like to listen to you.

Please, can you tell me what you think of this book.

What did you like?

What are you interested to learn more about?

What can I do for you?

You can do it from your phone or your computer by visiting https://www.karllillrud.com/hacking-your-destiny/feedback

This is not the end, this is the beginning!